Salvation

Salvation

*Scenes from the Life
of St. Francis*

VALERIE MARTIN

ALFRED A. KNOPF

NEW YORK

2001

THIS IS A BORZOI BOOK
PUBLISHED BY ALFRED A. KNOPF

www.aaknopf.com

Knopf, Borzoi Books, and the colophon are registered trademarks
of Random House, Inc.

Portions of this work originally appeared in slightly different form in
Atlantic Monthly and *The New Orleans Review.*

Library of Congress Cataloging-in-Publication Data
Martin, Valerie.
Salvation : scenes from the life of St. Francis / Valerie Martin.—1st ed.
p.   cm.
Includes bibliographical references.
ISBN 0-375-40983-1
1. Francis, of Assisi, Saint, 1182–1226.   2. Christian saints—Italy—Assisi—
Biography.   3. Assisi (Italy)—Biography.   I. Title.
BX4700 F6 M35145 2001
271.302—dc21
[B]
00-044361

Manufactured in the United States of America
First Edition

The author would like to thank Prof. Julian Wasserman for reading and commenting on an early draft of this book, as well as Sr. Marianne Zadorzny of St. Clare's Monastery in New Orleans, for her enthusiastic response and for a glimpse of what St. Francis's vision looks like in the world today. To other friends who listened and encouraged me through vicissitudes of research and composition, especially Chris Wiltz, Melanie McKay, Jason Berry, Susan Larsen, and Christopher Benfey, warm thanks are due.

To John Cullen, who is still listening, to my agent, Nikki Smith, and my editor, Robin Desser, for their generous support and patience, I am most sincerely grateful. To my daughter Adrienne, who shared with me, one chilly afternoon in November, an extremely spooky experience at St. Francis's crypt in Assisi, my thanks for her continuing willingness to join me on all flights, real and imaginary.

But in these days there are many among us who want to win honor and praise from men by merely proclaiming and reciting the deeds of Saints.

—ST. FRANCIS OF ASSISI
Mirror of Perfection

Contents

Contents

Chronology

The Children's Crusade: several thousand
children meet at Vendôme, following the
boy leader Stephen   1212

The Fourth Lateran Council: Innocent
calls the Fifth Crusade   1215

Innocent III dies suddenly in Perugia   1216

Pontificate of Honorius II   1216–1227

Francesco travels to Syria; the fall
of Damietta   1219

At the Pentecost Chapter meeting,
Francesco resigns and appoints Pietro
di Catania vicar general of the order   1220
                                                  (or 1221)

Elia appointed vicar general of the order
at death of Pietro di Catania   1221

Francesco receives the stigmata at
Mount La Verna   1224 (September 14)

Francesco receives treatment for his
eye ailment at Rieti   1225

Resting at San Damiano, Francesco
composes the *Canticle of Brother Sun*   1225
                                                  (or 1226)

Francesco dies at the Portiuncula   1226 (October 3 or 4)

Pontificate of Pope Gregory IX,
formerly Ugolino di Segni   1227–1241

Francesco canonized at Assisi   1228 (July 16)

Transfer of Francesco's body
to the Basilica   1230 (May 25)

Salvation

Introduction

When San Francesco lay dying, he asked to be moved from the bishop's residence in Assisi to the chapel at the Portiuncula, a distance of about two miles outside the city walls. As they passed the city gates, he bid the friars carrying him to set him down on the road so that he might say farewell to the place of his birth. "This town," he began, "has the worst reputation in the whole region as the home of every kind of rogue and scoundrel." Then he begged God to bless the place and to make it the home of all who sincerely honored his name.

According to the brochure put out by the Commune's busy tourist agency, Assisi is a city that cannot just be "seen," it must be "experienced," a place, perhaps *the* place, where "the spirit of St. Francis pervades all." Every year hundreds of thousands of visitors, art lovers, tourists, and pilgrims from all over the world flock to see the famous basilica where the saint is buried. The narrow streets in which Francesco begged for bread are lined with hundreds of shops selling all manner of atrocious trinkets and some of the worst food to be found in Italy, at prices as breathtaking as the view from the Rocca Maggiore, the late-medieval fortress that glowers over the prosperous town. The spirit that pervades these streets is the same one that whistled down the stone staircases and across the Piazza del Commune in Francesco's lifetime, the same spirit that drove him straight into the outspread arms of Christ: the cold, relentless, insatiable, furious spirit of commerce.

Francesco di Pietro Bernardone was born in Assisi toward the end of 1181, the son of a wealthy cloth merchant, Pietro Bernardone, and his wife, Pica, who may or may not have been French. Francesco had an ordinary childhood, helping with his father's business and attending the church school near their house, where he was an unremarkable student. He grew to be a lively young man, fond of music and parties, given to romantic tales, dreams of knighthood, fantastic treasure quests, and prayer in solitary chapels. During one such occasion, at the dilapidated Church of San Damiano, God spoke to him from a crucifix, bidding him to repair the church. Francesco took some bolts of cloth from his father's warehouse, sold them, and delivered the profit to the resident priest to pay for the repair of the chapel. Pietro, enraged by his son's extravagance, brought a complaint against him, which was resolved in the public square of Assisi. When the bishop advised Francesco to return the money to his father, he declared, "My Lord Bishop, not only will I gladly give back the money which is my father's but also my clothes." He stripped off his clothes, placed the money on them, and, standing naked before the bishop, his father, and all present, announced, "Listen, all of you, and mark my words. Hitherto I have called Pietro Bernardone my father; but because I am resolved to serve God I return to him the money on account of which he was so perturbed, and also the clothes I wore which are his; and from now on I will say, 'Our father who art in heaven,' and not Father Pietro Bernardone." The crowd wept in sympathy, and the bishop covered the youth with his own cloak.

Francesco then took refuge in the poor church, where he devoted himself to making repairs, begging for food, oil, and stones on the streets of Assisi. His former neighbors mocked him and drove him away, but one rich young man, Bernardo of Quintavalle, impressed by Francesco's sincerity and evident contentment in his new life, decided to join him. Together the two men gave away all of Bernardo's money and possessions to the poor.

After that, there were more followers. In 1209, when they numbered eleven, the group walked to Rome to ask the pope to approve a Rule by which they might live as liegemen to the Church. After a dream in which he saw the Lateran Basilica collapsing and Francesco holding it up, the pope, Innocent III, gave them a verbal and very conditional approval.

Francesco's brotherhood, the Fratres Minores, grew rapidly. Within a few years, the original twelve had grown to five thousand (by contrast, the Dominican order, the Friars Preachers, as they were known, founded at roughly the same time, had fewer than fifty friars by 1220), and they gathered each year during the feast of Pentecost for chapter meetings at the Portiuncula, a wooded area owned by local Benedictine monks and leased to the friars for one basket of fish per year. At these meetings, Francesco delivered various admonitions, the friars were assigned to different regions, the *custos* and ministers were appointed, and problems of administration were addressed. Between these meetings, the mission of the *fratres* was to wander homeless over the world, preaching repentance, begging for their food, offering themselves as servants to all. This was the way, they believed, the early apostles had lived, the way Christ had adjured all his followers to live, giving the world an example of virtue, loving poverty, making no preparations for the next meal, the next bed, but leaving everything to God.

San Francesco's ministry lasted nearly twenty years. His health was never good. In Egypt, where he went to attempt the conversion of the sultan, he contracted an eye disease that made his eyes weep continuously, gave him such terrific headaches that he could not stand any light, and eventually left him blind. He gave up the stewardship of the order and retired to Mount La Verna with three of his closest friends for a period of fasting and prayer. When he came down from this mountain, he had two features that distinguished him from all previous saints: his hands and feet were pierced by nails and there was an open wound in his side, as from a lance.

With the possible exception of St. Paul, who wrote in his Epistle to the Galatians (6:17), "I bear in my body the marks of the

Lord Jesus," San Francesco's was the first recorded occurrence of the stigmata. It is not an exaggeration to say that the stigmata, as a religious phenomenon, was his idea. How such a thing could happen is, naturally, a great mystery, and before that mystery, many of his biographers come to a grinding halt, as if, rounding a bend in their pursuit of the humble saint, they suddenly encountered a raging elephant. Some see this event as the crowning achievement of Francesco's life, signaling his complete identification, hence, union, with his beloved Christ. Others suggest that there was an element of despair in the miracle; that Francesco saw himself as one crucified by the unrest and infighting in the great movement he had founded. His contemporaries, though they had never heard of such a thing, seem to have accepted it and found it in keeping with what they understood to be the nature of God's continual interference in the world of men. In their view, Francesco had been singled out and marked by Christ as his own. The stigmata proved what everyone already suspected, that he was a living saint. Two years later, in October 1226, Francesco died peacefully at Assisi, revered by all, his devoted friars gathered around him. He was forty-five years old.

This is the story one can follow in the fresco cycles painted by some of the greatest artists of the Italian Renaissance—Cimabue, Giotto, Sassetta, Bellini, Gozzoli—in colors and compositions that, after hundreds of years, retain an astonishing freshness and a heady exuberance, as if the artists were excited about the story they were telling. Unconcerned with meaning, they throw their energy into a personal vision, concentrating on atmosphere. Each sees the saint differently (Gozzoli, for example, contrary to several descriptions given by people who saw Francesco, paints him as a handsome, healthy young man with curling golden locks), and each brings the considerable force of his artistry to bear on "the life." They know the stories, are of the environment that produced the saint, speak the language he spoke, and believe, more or less, what he believed. The humble friar wandering silently through the landscape of the frescoes, his head encircled by light, is thus both a construct and a memory.

San Francesco is the patron saint of Italy, and nearly every town has a church in his name, decorated with scenes from his life; but the first cycle I saw was in the National Gallery of London nearly fifteen years ago. It was painted by a Sienese artist known as Il Sassetta sometime in the fifteenth century. I had seen prints of it, and had for many years a framed detail of the panel entitled *The Mystical Marriage of St. Francis* over my desk; it shows St. Francis exchanging wedding rings with Lady Poverty, a pretty barefoot girl with a wooden yoke over her shoulders. (I thought, as a young writer, I might profit by a daily colloquy with this lady.) But prints did not prepare me for the strangeness, the avidity, of the actual paintings. Fortunately, there was a bench in front of them, and I sat there for some time, admiring the otherworldly view.

When I moved to Italy in 1994, I made it a practice to visit any church or monastery that was reputed to have good frescoes of San Francesco. I was particularly drawn to the cycle painted by Benozzo Gozzoli in Montefalco, which depicts the saint as the new Christ, even reworking the nativity so that he takes his first breath amid cattle (though we know San Francesco was not born in a stable). In these paintings, as in the Sassetta cycle, the saint moves through a world that is both ordinary and magical. He lies comfortably on his bed while an angel enters the room from the ceiling, and outside his window, his dream—a castle with flying pennants—rises into the middle air. In another panel, he rushes down the street before his house, a well-dressed youth in a hurry, about to be waylaid by a poor man who prophesies that he will be a great saint. From the doorway, Francesco's mother looks on with an expression of mild foreboding.

The various frescoes drew my attention to the character of San Francesco; a lifelong interest in hagiography did the rest. I began to pick up biographies, randomly at first, and then with more direction, finding myself returning to the earliest sources, the accounts collected by the saint's three closest friends: Brother Leone, who served as his secretary for the last years of his life, and Brothers Rufino and Angelo, who were with him in the early days of the order.

Because saints were presumed to have certain agreed-upon powers and peculiarities, medieval hagiography has a tendency to emphasize the sameness of its subjects. Saints, for example, routinely possessed the ability to communicate with and tame wild animals. (St. Columban, an Irish saint who died within two hundred miles of Assisi, was known for his preaching to birds.) The oft-illustrated, well-loved stories of Francesco taming the wolf of Gubbio and preaching to the birds are probably apocryphal, intended to place him among a select company. Edward Armstrong points out one variant of the bird sermon story that strikes me as quite plausible, however. In this one, Francesco's preaching is ignored by the birds, who fly away, and he then chastises himself for being so vain as to imagine they would listen to him. This version has the ring of truth both because of the way Francesco chooses to reprimand himself—he calls himself "You stupid son of Pietro di Bernardone"—and the likelihood that he might want to try his hand at something saints were generally expected to do, for there can be no doubt that Francesco had every intention of becoming a saint.

But, in spite of their fidelity to the form of the inspirational text, the early hagiographies of San Francesco differ from accounts of other medieval saints. They contain surprising, small personal details (the saint's fondness for sweets, or the fact that his eyebrows met over the bridge of his nose), and represent a concerted effort to write down the exact manner and tone of his speech. The authors, who were with the saint for years on end, keep track of his moods and lament over his illnesses, complaining of the doctors' inability to do anything but make him worse. One has a sense of their urgency to get down for posterity this remarkable personality which was unlike any they had ever known. They quote Francesco confidently, not reverentially, and with an ear to the incisive wit and irony that surprised all those who knew him.

A second difference in these accounts is more difficult to describe, because it is more a matter of tone than content, an insistence that borders on stridency—as if the saint needed defending, as if there was an accusation to answer, as if San Francesco was on trial. This defensiveness on the part of his biographers persists to the present and can be explained in part by the events just preceding and following his death, for, though he died peacefully, in the odor of sanctity, the steely charge of controversy was in the air as well.

Before he died, the order San Francesco founded had begun to self-destruct—a fact that poisoned the last years of his life. As soon as he was gone, the Fratres Minores split into two factions that viewed each other with distrust and contempt. The crucial issue was Francesco's insistence, repeated in the various Rules he composed during his lifetime and with much force in his final testament, dictated on his deathbed, that the friars were to own no property, either personal or communal, excepting "one habit, quilted inside and out if they wished, with a cord and breeches."

In 1228, barely two years after his death, San Francesco was canonized by Pope Gregory IX (formerly Cardinal Ugolino of Segni, Francesco's old friend and patron of the order). The cornerstone was laid at Assisi, and Brother Elia, then minister general of the order, began the excavation for the great basilica in which the saint was to be buried. To this end, Brother Elia solicited and received in abundance that which Francesco had forbidden the friars even to touch: money.

Two years later, in September 1230, in the bull *Quo elongati*, Pope Gregory decreed that the testament, because it had been written without the consent of the minister general, had no binding power over the order. The friars could not *own* property, but they could have *use* of property owned by someone else—for example, the pope. They could, then, establish houses; have the use of books and furniture; rely on a supply of food; and attend the universities in Bologna and Paris. So fearful was the reaction to this decree in the widespread brotherhood (by this time some twenty thousand strong) that Francesco's earliest companions, Rufino, Angelo, and Egidio, were forced to go into hiding to escape persecution.

From the start, Francesco's biographers have been forced to address this controversy, to take sides, defending either the Church, which acted to preserve peace inside the order and to guarantee its continuance and governability, or Francesco, ignored and traduced by weak-minded followers who refused the rigor of his rule and betrayed his most treasured principle, the vow of total poverty. The fact that Francesco was also adamantly submissive to the Church, and especially to the pope, adds a certain piquancy to the struggle to settle the question of whether the founder actually intended to create anything resembling the order that bears his name. Evidently, he saw no conflict between his determination to respect Church authority and his need to follow the dictates of his own conscience, which he believed was in direct communication with God. He saw no contradiction even when these two were at loggerheads. Like a soldier who understands the chain of command, he took his orders from anyone who was over him, but when the battle raged and the general appeared on the field, he knew what to do.

The idea of poverty as essential to salvation was not original to Francesco. In the twelfth and thirteenth centuries, the "poverty movement" was afoot, or more correctly barefoot, all over Europe. The Cathars, the Waldensians, the Reclusi, the Humiliati, the Beghards, the Apostolic Brethren, the Paterini—to name just a few—were all sects, perhaps today we would call them cults, dedicated in varying degrees and with various concomitant, often heretical, articles of faith (the Cathars, for example, held that the material world was made by the devil and hence entirely evil) to the ideal of living as the early apostles of Jesus had lived—on the road. Presumably, this was a reaction against the increasingly flamboyant wealth and scandalous behavior of the clergy. It derived as well from an assumption that has lost ground over the centuries but was held as obvious in the medieval world, that the material and spiritual realms are intimately connected, and that we concentrate on one at the expense of the other. The accumulation of wealth created a spiritual obligation; thus the great medieval churches were largely financed by rich men who hoped to compensate God for their sins by creating more and more fabulous houses for his worship.

The connection between destitution and virtue is largely lost upon us now, especially, it seems to me, in America, where poverty is so clearly unconstitutional that we once declared war upon it. The notion that one must choose between spiritual and material "success" is in disfavor as well. In fact, all sorts of popular venues, from self-help books to TV evangelists, suggest that if you can only place yourself before the proper spiritual door, when you open it, money will pour in. It is surprising how often successful people, from jockeys to business executives, attribute their material success to some proper alliance with God, as if God really did take an interest in the stock market or bet the horses. Perhaps the assumption that God wants us to get rich is no more absurd than the one Francesco made, that he wants us poor, that he wants us to suffer, as he did, the contempt of the world. But there's nothing heroic, in my view, about praying for a windfall, whereas there is something heroic, touching, and grand about Francesco's famous gesture, stripping himself in the town square and throwing himself upon the charity of his neighbors. Like most of us, Francesco knew his neighbors.

Francesco's apprehension of the zeitgeist was unusual in that it was direct and uncomplicated—there were no complex additions to his theology or divergence from the accepted practice of religion in his day—as well as profoundly personal and deeply felt. As a young man, he committed himself to a humiliating, onerous way of life, and until his death, though he was encouraged by the Church hierarchy (and even by his own brotherhood) to modify his radical devotion to "Holy Poverty," he never wavered in that commitment. He was a great success because he was determined to be, in the world's eye, a perfect failure.

Apart from the interest his history arouses in me, I do not have a special connection to San Francesco. I am not a believer in miracles; rather, I hold that the laws of nature apply even to those who know nothing about them. I am not a scholar of his period, not an Italian—nor can I read Italian or Latin with ease—not a Roman Catholic or particularly religious; I am not even a man.

I do believe, as he did, that the relationship between material prosperity and spiritual progress is nil, and I know that for those who are convinced the most salient fact of our existence is the certainty that we must leave it, spirituality, by which I mean the apprehension of another (not necessarily an after-) life, offers egress from a prison. Such an apprehension reveals that true liberation has nothing to do with physical comfort or the accumulation of wealth (for wealth, as we readily observe, can crush the spirit) but rather with a willingness to turn away from the mundane business of daily life, to abandon everything ordinary, seeking instead an extraordinary course that will result in a coherent and meaningful confrontation with one's own death. Death then becomes not a trap set out somewhere in the obscure forest of the future, where we wander hopeless with uncertain steps, but the vanishing point of every day, which provides perspective, orders the chaos of experience, and is the proper object and goal of life.

As I rubbed my stiff neck, gazing up at the Gozzoli frescoes in Montefalco, I was touched by the artist's ability to show that, though San Francesco had an extraordinary life, it was, after all, a life like any other, lived in the world among men and women, buildings, beasts, and trees. This vision suited its subject, for though San Francesco was a great mystic, he was also entirely of this world. He was not so much a nature lover (he was certainly neither an environmentalist nor a vegetarian) as a man who saw no distinction between himself and the natural world. He preferred to live as an animal lives, rising with the sun, walking around all day looking for food, socializing with his own kind, sleeping on the ground with a stone for his pillow.

San Francesco's life, I concluded, requires neither defense nor interpretation. It occurred to me that his story might be best presented in a series of scenes, beginning in the dark, final days, so full of physical suffering and the adulation of the mob, and concluding in the bright clear light of his conversion, when he was a young man with all his possibilities before him. By this method I hope to offer a somewhat personal, alternative exhibit of scenes from the life.

From what I have been able to learn about him, San Francesco viewed this world largely as a placement test for the next. Like any brilliant and willing student, he was entirely absorbed in the business of the test. He began by concentrating the enormous energy of his will upon his own salvation, but by the time he died, he intended to lead a multitude into heaven and to take the next world by storm. His great work, as much a work of art as the many paintings and statues that celebrate it, was his life.

Like most tourists, when I sought out the paintings illustrating the life of San Francesco, I just wanted to see the art; the story was incidental. But that story, so sorrowful and triumphant, seemed to reach out from the walls and ceilings and grasp me by the shoulders. At Assisi, Montefalco, Florence, Rome, Arezzo, the ragged, barefoot beggar cried out to me: This is what I made of my life! Now go out and change your own!

On His Death

Night in the Forest

*And for morality life is a
war, and the service of the highest
is a sort of cosmic patriotism
which also calls for volunteers. Even a
sick man, unable to be militant
outwardly, can carry on the moral warfare.*

—WILLIAM JAMES
The Varieties of Religious Experience

Just before dawn, on a rough, unfrequented road east of Siena, a procession of barefoot friars makes a winding, difficult progress. Two lead the way, their cowls pushed back, their startled eyes shooting sparks of gold in the sputtering light of the torches they hold above their heads. Behind them, four of their brothers, each supporting a pole of a makeshift stretcher, stumble forward on the uneven stones. On the stretcher, wrapped in foul and bloody rags, lies a small, motionless body. No one speaks, but their labored breathing is audible in the still night air. As the road turns sharply uphill, the bearers shift their weight to accommodate the incline, and a low moan issues from the invalid. One of the torchbearers looks back, raising his hand to keep his beard from tangling in the folds of his cowl. He looks off to the side into the blackness that stretches against every bush, over every rock, like a tightly fitted stocking, and his eyes roll up momentarily, a reflex of fatigue and anxiety, for he has slept very little in the last few weeks and this is the most serious mission of his life.

They are to deliver the invalid, dead or alive, to Assisi, where Brother Elia waits impatiently, and all the citizens wait, too, in a great fever of anticipation and dread, lest their enemies steal their treasure away. The sick man must breathe his last inside the city walls, for wherever he expires is holy ground. A few nights ago it looked as if the proud city of Siena might claim this honor, for the dying man coughed blood, called on death, welcomed her, but she did not come. Toward morning the bleeding stopped, he closed his weary, sightless eyes and slept. A message went out to Assisi—he will not last much longer, and that was when Brother Elia sent the command: start at once, but stay clear of Perugia, for his enemies there have hatched a plot to steal him if they can, by stealth or ambush, so that he may die among them in the place he once cursed, and all the triumph, as well as the pilgrims, will be theirs.

The sick man acquiesced to the command, indeed could not resist; this going home to die was his wish as well. For one last night, the Sienese doctors practiced upon him. In their fury at losing him, they pierced his ears with hot irons and bled him until his veins gave out. In the morning, the brothers gathered to wash and prepare him for the long journey. His body terrified them. His feet and legs, which had been swollen for days, were stained blue and purple with bruises, and the swelling had spread to his abdomen. The rest of him, his chest, arms, neck, face, all was emaciated. Though he did not complain, he flinched beneath the wet cloths they pressed against him. He would not allow them to remove the filthy hair shirt which was glued with dried blood to his side. The wounds on his hands and feet were open and oozing; the brothers wrapped them tenderly in woundwort and strips of wool and applied a bandage to his forehead. Then they dressed him again in the dirty rags he had gotten from some beggar; he would have none other.

When they were finished, he raised his arms to grasp their shoulders as they lifted him from the floor. "Is this Brother Rufino?" he said, resting his cheek momentarily against a shoulder. Yes, he was right. As they laid him down, he reached out, and his fingers found the smooth cheek of another brother. "Brother Angelo," he said. His sightless eyes moved restlessly, unable to penetrate the shadows that hid the world from him.

They consulted over him, agreed upon their places, raised the litter, and carried him into the grand hall where the bishop waited to bid him a tearful farewell, then out through a low back door to a narrow passageway and down, down the winding stone stairs, past the shuttered, bolted housefronts, down to the city gate, where a band of beggars were quarreling in the dirt and soldiers stood about, yawning and stretching. A few tradesmen occupied in lashing their goods to the backs of tired donkeys failed to notice the passing band of friars.

Now out onto the plain they carry him, walking briskly over stones and thorns as they have walked for the last twenty years at the bidding of their invalid, six barefoot men in shabby, much-patched tunics, the soles of their feet as thick and tough as leather, their faces weathered and creased as gnarled trees, their heads bowed against the heat of the sun.

The route they have chosen is an arduous one, and they carry no provisions, but in the evening they stop at a place where others of their brotherhood await them and where they find food and mats to spread out on the ground for a few hours of rest. The invalid does not sleep; nor does he eat. He lies on his litter in the darkness among the snoring brothers, unable to move while the fluids in his body back up steadily: he can feel his skin stretching and stretching to the bursting point, like an overripe fruit. He can raise his bandaged hand to his temple, caress with his fingertips the thick, hard scars left by the irons the doctors applied at Fonte Colombo to no avail; nothing ever eases for one moment the fury of the pain in his head. The hours pass; they are endless, though surely now each one may be the last. Of that hour he has no fear, that hour when everything and everyone will be forgiven and he will bless the brotherhood finally and forever and say farewell, farewell, Brother Body, farewell, beautiful world. He can hear the night birds in the bushes, the fevered scratching of tiny claws on the hard ground, mice or moles, working out the eternal problem of shelter. He knows what it is to scratch for a place to sleep. Overhead are the stars and a sliver of moon, but he can't see them. A cloud lies against his eyes, or in his eyes. Sometimes there is a moment when he peers through it. It thins out, goes white like light, which hurts him, then an image appears in startling detail, like a shout in an otherwise silent room. Once he saw a section of pomegranate spilling its red seeds like glistening drops of blood across the polished black surface of a wooden plate; Leone had brought it to him from the bishop's table. Later, as they carried him along a forest path, a bright green leaf stabbed through the cloud so that he gasped as before an advancing sword-point; then, as suddenly as it had come, it was gone again. But in that instant he had recognized it: it was a mulberry leaf.

The long hours pass, the brothers snore and grumble in their sleep, then he hears them waking up around him one by one, muttering and coughing, greeting one another, chanting the office, though it is still the middle of the night and prayers are not strictly required. Leone brings him water and asks if he can eat anything. He hears the others laughing as they gather up their straw beds and share out the bread and turnips the resident brothers have brought them. More bounty, more than anyone could ask for, and all provided from the never-ending bounty of God. He cannot eat. He asks for cool cloths to bathe his eyes, which feel like twin flames in his head, and Masseo comes with a bowl of water to help Leone. He hears the whoosh and hiss and feels the hot sulfurous breath of fire as the torches go up, and then the salutations of his four bearers who take their places and lift him up for the last leg of his long journey back to the city of his birth.

Into the forest, into the darkness, anxious and vigilant, the procession moves like a glittering thread among the trees. They keep silence, the better to hear an ambush approaching. Birds screech overhead; they flush out a bevy of pheasants and a rabbit. A deer crashing through the underbrush never sees the wide eyes or hears the racing hearts of the frozen, nervous band. Dawn is nearing. The air grows damp, warm, and pellucid; their feet make a steady rhythm on the hard, dry ground. Downhill, now, the path grows wider, then pours them out onto a dusty plain. The torchbearers stop to extinguish their flames in the dirt of the roadbed. A murmur goes up among them as they turn their faces toward the distant towers and walls of Assisi and see, winding toward them over the farthest hill like a great, gleaming snake in the early morning mist, a contingent of soldiers, the archers of the Commune of Assisi, coming out to meet them.

Someone tells the invalid, who cannot see the marvelous sight. They lay him down in the fragrant shade of a pine tree and gather to watch the approach of the escort, and to tell him how the shields glitter like jewels in the morning sun, how the banners stream out over the foot soldiers, how black and proud the horses are, tossing their heads and stamping their hooves, how white the saddles and colorful the embroidered mantles of the knights. Over the first hill they come, and then, for a little while, they disappear into a valley. The friars stand together, straining their eyes, craning their necks, swatting dully at the buzzing mosquitoes. Before the soldiers appear again, the brothers can hear them—a shout has gone up, followed by a raucous, unsuccessful attempt at song, which fades out amid more shouting and laughter.

As the soldiers top the last hill, they see the friars hovering like brooding gray birds over the exhausted invalid, who lies on the ground with his bandaged hands over his eyes because the light is agony for him. At a command from one of the glorious knights, the foot soldiers tuck in their bows close to their sides and break into a trot, raising a cloud of dust that rolls out ahead of the close-knit ranks like a dragon's fiery breath.

Soon the two groups, friars and soldiers, mingle on the verge of the forest. Now there is nothing to fear; their enemies will not dare to attack them. The knights mill among their bowmen, giving orders. One speaks courteously to Brother Angelo, who was once a knight and has still a noble bearing. Excitement agitates the group, and they bump into one another as the procession is organized, knights to the front and back, archers between and flanking the friars, and in the center, the dying man. When they get to the Commune, they will have to defend him from the citizens, who will snatch whatever they can, a bit of his robe, hairs from his beard. It is said that a straw from the hay he touched at a crib in Greccio cured a child near death, as well as an entire herd of ailing cows. The archers re-form their lines; the horses step out, their eyes rolling wildly, their black lips dripping pale green foam; the brothers gather about the litter and lift it; the torchbearers take their places on either side.

The dying man has not spoken. One hand still covers his eyes. They carry him to the center of the group, an order is shouted and repeated, the banners go up, the archers, sweating and red-faced, fall into step, the procession begins. Anyone watching from the ruins of the castle that broods over the city can see the sun glancing off the shiny helmets, the knot of bright colors wrapped around the plain gray core of the friars, the whole assembly moving steadily along the dark ribbon of the road, hemmed in on one side by the gold of a grain field and on the other by the smoky green of an olive grove. A noble sight. Even the friars, who have vowed never to put themselves above any man, stride boldly, their shoulders back, their heads held high. One of them has moved to the front, where he exchanges a few words with the foremost bearer. Then he glances anxiously over his shoulder at the invalid, who, to his surprise, uncovers his eyes and raises his hand in a summons. The friar drops back, falls into step, and looks down upon his dying friend. How illness has ravaged this face; he is scarcely recognizable. The black eyes are embedded in red, swollen flesh; otherwise, he is as gray as his robe, and the bones of his skull protrude beneath his skin at his cheeks, above his mouth, and in a ridge that divides his forehead. Yet, to his astonishment, as the brother watches, this death's head is suddenly, eerily animated. Francesco's eyes move from side to side, his dry, cracked lips part, and then, as he grasps his disciple's hand, he smiles. It is not the helpless grimace of a man in agony, which is surely his condition, but an open, lighthearted, youthful smile, confident, a touch sardonic, but full of camaraderie. "Ah, ah, Brother Leone," he says, as his old friend bends over him.

Leone looks up then, his hand in the firm grasp of the invalid, and through a wash of tears sees the proud backs of the knights rising above the swishing tails and sweating haunches of their horses, and he hears the steady pounding of all the many feet, some shod in iron, some in leather, and some—his own—unshod. This is a triumphant procession. When they enter the city gates, the people will be there, shoving and shouting, "Il Santo, il Santo." Elia will welcome them at the stone portals of the bishop's palace, the guards will take their posts, the brothers will not be eating bread and turnips tonight but delicacies from the bishop's table: salted fish, pheasants stuffed with raisins, hares in fennel sauce, quinces, almonds, and fine wine. The beggars will be the lords and the lord of the beggars will be the Lord of all. All will be just as it should be, which is what Leone has read in Francesco's smile.

They file on, not hurried but insistent, like a ship flying its pennants on a favorable current of water and air. The sun is up; it pours over them. The day is unseasonably warm. Mosquitoes and flies buzz around their heads, dust rises and settles in their noses and teeth. They pass the rotting carcass of a horse, its body defined by a loud, buzzing wedge of flies that rises over the ditch where it has fallen. The long neck and eyeless head stretch out into the road, as if to gaze upon the gallant parade passing by. Overhead, in the pale sky, two vultures circle patiently.

A Last Request

What separates us from antiquity and the Middle Ages is the fact that we no longer know how to prepare ourselves for death. No one cultivates death in himself any longer, it happens over and above him.

—E. M. CIORAN
Tears and Saints

How much neglect and abuse can a body endure? Francesco is the dying proof—only so much, and then there is a revolt in all its parts. All night at the bishop's house, Francesco has vomited blood, and then all morning dark green bile. He does not retch or struggle, but only opens his mouth, and out it pours in such quantities that the brothers perfect a system using three bowls, passing empty to full, from the patient to the bucket. Between bouts, Francesco clutches Leone's arm and whispers long, unintelligible commands. He is fervent, insistent. Leone looks about helplessly. Rufino leans over the invalid, bringing his ear to the muttering lips, but he can make no sense of it. No one can.

When at last Francesco sleeps, they hardly dare speak for fear of waking him. The hours pass, they hear the bells for matins, they mouth their prayers in silence, and then Francesco wakes up and he is as clear as a mountain pool and intent upon dictation. Sitting on the floor with a stool for his writing desk, Leone flattens his parchment and dips his pen. For a long time the only sounds are Francesco's voice, weak yet as unwavering as if reciting a memorized text, and the scratching of Leone's pen. "This is how God inspired me, Brother Francesco, to embark upon a life of penance. When I was in sin, the sight of lepers nauseated me beyond measure."

He goes all the way back: this is how it began, his horror of lepers. Then he speaks of how God gave him friars but no one told him what to do, of their visit to the Lord Pope in Roma, the pope's approval, his own simple plan, too simple now, he knows that, but he clings to it most of all. "They were satisfied with one habit which was patched inside and out, and a cord, and breeches. We refused to have anything more." He pauses. Leone dips his pen. Rufino moistens Francesco's lips with a cloth. "I am determined," he continues, "to obey the minister general of the order and the guardian whom he sees fit to give me. I want to be a captive in his hands so that I cannot travel about or do anything against his command or desire, because he is my superior. Although I am ill and not much use, I always want to have a cleric with me who will say the office for me, as is prescribed in the Rule." He reminds them that any friar who fails to say the office according to the Rule should be put in prison until he can be judged by Cardinal Ugolino. He is dying, and he is thinking about prison. "In virtue of obedience, I strictly forbid any of my friars, clerics or lay brothers, to interpret the Rule or these words, saying 'This is what they mean.' God inspired me to write the Rule and these words plainly and simply, and so you too must understand them plainly and simply, and live by them, doing good to the last." His voice fades. He mumbles, speaking to some companion he imagines near his ear. His blind eyes wander, roll up, showing the whites; the lids close abruptly and his breath escapes in a puff.

Is he dead? Again Rufino leans over him, lowers his face to his lips. "He is living," he says. Leone blows upon the page, wipes his pen on his sleeve. "He is asleep."

But just as Rufino turns away, Francesco's eyes snap open, and he gasps noisily. His hands fly up, tear the air, then, before the astonished friars, he pulls himself into a sitting position and begins plucking at his robe frantically, drawing it up over his knees. Rufino tries to stay his hands, but Francesco bats him away forcefully without speaking. He works the robe up over his thin buttocks, then reaches over his head to pull it free from the back of his neck. He is naked now, for the brothers have removed his breeches to keep them from irritating his skin which is so thin he can be bruised by a touch. Free of the robe, he sits gravely for a moment, clutching the edge of the bed, his blind eyes staring at nothing. Rufino points out that the room is cold. He and Leone stand watching Francesco almost warily, as if he might be dangerous. Angelo studies the exposed wound in his side, red but closed, the raw flesh puckered into a circlet, like a tiny mouth. Francesco pats the stone floor with his bandaged feet, as if feeling about for something lost; then, abruptly, he lurches forward and throws himself facedown.

"Francesco," Leone says. He drops to his knees and reaches across the floor to his friend's flailing body. Francesco pushes himself up on one side, then, raising one hand as if to pull on some invisible bar, rolls over onto his back. He is still. His mouth opens, closes. He smiles. Rufino has taken up the discarded robe and clutches it to his chest. The brothers look at one another. What are they to do? If Francesco wants to lie naked on the cold stone floor, is it their duty to stop him? He has wanted more extraordinary things than this, and they have obeyed him, but now he is in their care, not they in his. Rufino is so rattled by the strangeness of it, Francesco there before him, smiling up into some world no one else can see, that tears start in his eyes. "Francesco," he pleads. "Take this robe which I lend to you. It is not yours to give away, but only to please me, because I am lending it to you, will you wear it?"

Francesco turns his face in the direction of Rufino's voice but makes no answer.

"Francesco," Leone says, his fingers touching the chilly shoulder of the invalid. "Rufino will lend you this robe to wear."

The smile disappears. He turns now toward Leone. "As you wish," he says.

They gather around him. Leone helps him to sit up, Rufino lifts one arm, and Angelo assists in working the heavy sleeve on, then over Francesco's bowed, silent head, then onto his other arm. He sits, slumped forward, his legs stuck out straight before him. His eyes seem to focus upon the bandages encircling his feet. In one motion, the friars lift him—he weighs nothing, he is only bones—

and slide him back onto the hard platform of the bed. At once he is asleep.

Later he awakes with a start. Rufino touches his arm and says, "Father, I am here."

"What day is it?" Francesco asks.

"It is Thursday," Leone replies.

"I thought it was Friday."

The friars look at one another, but none speaks.

"When you see that I am in my last moments," Francesco says, "place me naked on the floor, just as you saw me the day before yesterday, and let me lie there after I am dead for the time it takes a man to walk a mile unhurriedly." His voice is calm, as if he is planning one of their journeys together, a walk to Gubbio, perhaps, or to Nocera, where it is always cool. His audience is silent. Rufino presses the damp cloth against the patient's forehead.

"Promise me," Francesco says.

"Father," Leone replies. "It will be just as you say."

"Good," Francesco says. He dabs at his ceaselessly weeping eye with his bandaged hand. "Bring some ashes," he says. "Sprinkle them over me now."

Leone takes a bowl from the stone table and goes to the flickering fire near the door. Squatting before it, he uses a bit of kindling to rake the still-warm ashes into the bowl.

Elia's Joyful Message

When Christians stop confessing that they are sinners, unprofitable servants, and to that extent that they are not Christians, the Christian faith ends.

—JOHN GARVEY
Daily Readings with St. Francis of Assisi

To Brother Gregory, beloved in Christ, minister of the brethren in France, and to all of his and our brethren, greetings from Brother Elia, a sinner.

Before I begin to write, I must give expression to my sorrow, and indeed I have reason to do so. As overflowing waters, so is my grief. For the fear I feared has come upon me and upon you, and that which I was afraid of has befallen me and you.

The comforter is far from us, and he who carried us like lambs in his arms has departed into a strange and distant country.

Beloved of God and men, he has been taken up into brightly shining mansions—he who taught Jacob the law of life and conduct and gave to Israel the covenant of peace.

For his sake we should rejoice exceedingly, but for us there must needs be sorrow; without him darkness envelops us, and the shadows of death enshroud us.

If it is a great loss for all, it is fraught with particular danger for me whom he left behind in the midst of darkness, oppressed and harried on all sides by countless anxieties.

Hence I beseech you, brethren, weep with me who am immersed in deep sorrow.

We are orphans without a father; we have lost the light of our eyes. Verily, our Brother and Father Francesco was a true light to us, to those near us, and also to those who were not associated with him by vocation and manner of life.

He was a light, sent by the true Light, to shine on those who sit in darkness and in the shadow of death, and to guide their feet into the way of peace. This he did in as far as the true Sun, the Orient from on high (that is, Christ) illuminated his heart and inflamed his will.

With ardent love he announced the kingdom of God, imbued the children with the thoughts and sentiments of the fathers, taught the incredulous the wisdom of the just, and prepared unto the Lord a perfect people in the whole world.

Even to the islands far off, his name went abroad, and all lands praise his wonderful deeds.

For this reason, sons and brothers, do not yield to excessive grief, for God the Father of orphans will console us with His holy consolation. When you weep, brethren, weep for yourselves, not over him. For we, who are sojourning among the living, are in death, whereas he went from death to life.

Rejoice since he, another Jacob, blessed all his sons before he was taken from us, and he forgave all of us who may have been guilty of some offence against him in thought or deed.

I take this occasion also to communicate to you very joyful news—a new miracle. Never yet has anyone heard of such wondrous signs except in the case of the Son of God, who is Christ the Lord.

For, a long time before his death, our Brother and Father Francesco was visibly crucified; he bore on his body the five wounds, the genuine stigmata of Christ. His hands and feet were pierced through as by nails; they retained these wounds and showed the black color of nails. His side was opened as by a lance and bled frequently.

As long as his soul still was in the body, he was not handsome of appearance; but his countenance was unattractive, and none of the members of his body was spared acute sufferings. As a result of the contraction of his muscles, his limbs were stiff like those of a dead person.

But now that he has died he is lovely to behold, he shines with a wonderful brilliance, and he causes all who look upon him to rejoice. His limbs, formerly stiff, are flexible and can be arranged in any position just as those of a delicate child.

Brethren, bless ye, therefore, the God of Heaven, give glory everywhere to Him who hath shown mercy to us.

Remember our Brother and Father Francesco until the glory of God, who has made him great among men and has exalted him above the angels. Pray for him, as he asked of us, and pray to him that God may grant us His holy grace even as He granted it to him.

On the eve of Sunday, October the fourth, one hour after sunset, our Father and Brother Francesco departed from us and went to Christ.

When you, dearest Brethren, receive this letter, imitate the people of Israel as they wept over their great leaders, Moses and Aaron. We may permit our tears to flow freely—we who have lost the consolation of such a Father!

It is a pious thing to rejoice with Francesco, but it is pious also to weep over him.

Of a truth it is pious to rejoice with Francesco, for, he has not died, since (in the morning) he went away to the market of heaven, carrying with him a purse full of money (his merits), and in the evening he will come back.

It is pious to weep over Francesco, for, he who went about as did Aaron, who presented to us both new and old gifts out of his treasury, who consoled us in every trial—he has been taken from our midst, and we are orphans without a father.

But it is written: To thee is the poor man left: thou wilt be a helper to the orphan.

Most beloved brethren, all of you, pray perseveringly that, after the little earthly vessel has been broken in the vale of the children of Adam, that highest Master-Potterer may provide another new, brightly shining vessel, who will preside over our numerous brotherhood and, like a true Maccabean, will lead us on to battle.

Since it is not in vain to pray for the dead, pray to the Lord for his soul. Every priest shall read three Masses, every cleric shall pray the Psalter, the lay brothers the Pater Noster five times, and the clerics shall solemnly chant Matins in choir. Amen.

Brother Elia, a sinner.

Elia Closes the Door

Alas, if this still lived from its own flame and were not only kept up from heart to heart laboriously, how different would be the intensity in the intimate lower church.

—RAINER MARIA RILKE
Letters 1910–1926

They have rolled the stone from the tomb and now are pulling the poor coffin up from its resting place at San Giorgio. As the workmen struggle with the ropes, they can hear Francesco's corpse sliding from side to side. Outside on the bright piazza the crowd has already gathered, and the whole route to the new basilica is lined with eager citizens. Girolamo, the podesta, stands in the nave smoothing the vair on his stiff, silk-lined cap. He was a witness to the miraculous stigmata of the saint, and it is said that he moved the nails back and forth through the wounded feet and cried out when he touched the still-moist wound in Francesco's most holy side.

The friars mill about the coffin, reciting their endless prayers. One carries a cloth woven of blood-red silk, embroidered by the Poor Ladies in threads of silver and gold, which they have offered to serve as a pall for this last journey of their holy father.

Since Francesco's death, the Commune has thrived on his legend. Two years ago, the Lord Pope and his cardinals came to declare Father Francesco a saint and to lay the cornerstone for the basilica to be built in his praise, which the minister Elia has designed to house both the dead saint and the living order. That was a day of triumph, when great counts, prelates, and religious from all over the world, even Jean of Brienne who was king of Jerusalem, came to honor this holy man. The Lord Pope was arrayed all in gold, his gold tiara encrusted with sparkling jewels, and the cardinals were all in white robes and miters, so as they stood in the bright sun on the green lawn—called in ancient times the hill of hell but renamed on this day the hill of paradise—they shone like God and his angels come to earth to accept a new saint into their celestial communion. Now that green lawn is an impenetrable forest of scaffolding, pulleys, and winches of all description, great piles of rock and marble, all shrouded in a permanent cloud of dust. But the vaulted ceiling is in place, the bronze doors are installed, and Brother Elia has declared the time has come to bring his beloved father to this far from peaceful, consecrated ground.

At the basilica, the doors open only on Elia's command, for he has prepared everything, as is his way, down to the smallest detail. In this the friars indulge him, for he was placed in authority by Father Francesco himself, but rumors fly and protests make their way down the long valley to the marble steps of the Holy See. "All you need now is wives," Brother Egidio observed when he toured the place and Elia showed him the plans for the *convento*, humiliating Elia before his workers and earning his enmity forever.

A man of great energy and action, Brother Elia paces nervously in the apse as the coffin clears the dark hole and the brothers swing it into place upon the bier. Girolamo approaches Brother Elia and speaks to him quietly, while the workmen brush the clods of clay from the coffin and Brother Leone covers it with the shimmering cloth.

The bier is an elaborate concoction of ivory and onyx, carved with scenes from Christ's passion and fitted with raised grips on the sides and two wooden poles, black and smooth as stone, extending past the corners. The friars take their places, awaiting Elia's command. In the vestibule the young men of the Commune chatter amiably as they unfurl their colorful flags; the two who carry the drums try out the solemn beat with which they will attempt to measure the enthusiasm of the crowd. Outside, some choristers have begun chanting new verses in praise of the stigmata, while others content themselves with calling out Francesco's name. Elia and Girolamo continue their conversation, though Elia is also occupied in tying a black scarf about his head. "Il Santo," someone shouts, pounding the closed door with his fist, and then another takes up the cry and pounds the door as well. Elia studies the coffin. They will want to see him, whatever is left of him. It would be better if that box were made of iron.

He nods once at the friars, who raise their hands to the bier, and he turns to the drummer gesticulating at the doors which vibrate with the blows and shouts of the mob. "Open the doors," Elia commands.

The friars take their places around the coffin, lifting it onto their shoulders. A workman pulls the bolt, and the crowd bursts through the doors with a shout of joy. Light pours into the dark church so that the drummer squints as he steps into the lead. Laughing and calling out to one another, the young men snap their flags into the leather cups attached to their thick belts. They step out boldly onto the glittering stone. Elia and Girolamo, their hands clasped at their waists, their faces solemn and suspicious, follow, standing for a moment to look out over the wild enthusiasm of the crowd, then they, too, step into the light. Now the friars appear in the doorway, stooped beneath their sacred burden, and the crowd lets out such a shout, "Il Santo, Il Santo," that they pause uncertainly, until Elia turns and urges them forward.

As the crowd presses in upon him, Elia flinches. He can hear the sound of rude hands slapping against the pall of the coffin. The city gate stands open before him, but it looks far away. He is torn between two desires, to bolt for the gate or to turn back and defend the coffin. The shouts and singing swell around him. Men and women clutch one another, executing brief, mad dances until the dust rises up around them like smoke from the doors of hell, and indeed they seem to Elia so many devils endangering his plan. He looks back at the brothers trudging beneath the coffin and sees in Leone's furtive glance something of the anxiety gripping his own heart. He speaks to Girolamo, who inclines his head to hear the order he has been waiting for, then takes off toward the gates at a run, his robe fluttering out behind him. The flag bearers are jostled and pressed by the crowd, but they are good-natured, elbowing their way forward, sweating and steaming in the merciless heat. No one wants a shred of their clothes, their living flesh and bones are safe enough, but Elia can hear the sound of hands rubbing and tapping the wood of the coffin behind him, and when he looks back again, he sees a friar lifting his arm to protect his head from a woman, her face tear-streaked, her mouth stretched wide in a grimace that might be joy or pain, who throws herself against the coffin, crying out, as her fingers tear at the pall, "Francesco, Francesco, return to us, save us, holy saint." Elia shudders and clutches his beard.

The flag bearers have nearly reached the gate. At any moment they will see what awaits them. The crowd waves olive branches; occasionally, puffs of flower petals burst over their heads, but this perfume is no match for the rank odor of the overheated citizens. Elia presses his sleeve against his nose, gazing over the city walls into the clear blue sky, where a whirling flock of swallows makes sharp black patterns, like writing, in the air. He hears a sound that rivets his attention to the gate: the metallic rattle of shields being shifted into place. The drummer has passed through and, to his credit, keeps up the funereal beat, even as the soldiers rush past him, bursting upon the crowd, their shields chest-high to make a gaily painted pushing wall. Now the shouts of joy, the ecstasy of singing, change to one long cry of outrage, for the soldiers charge into the crowd, surrounding the bier as ants alight upon a morsel of bread, in single lines from diverse directions.

The friars cry out, calling upon the bones they carry to defend them, but they are weak and easily wrested aside by the armed and powerful men. Elia has dropped behind the bier, observing with satisfaction the speed with which the soldiers flank it three thick, and how the crowd falls away as the coffin surges forward through the gate. The route is prearranged, along winding streets and narrow passageways where the mob will be forced to fall behind, then out across the greensward at a brisk pace, through the rubble of the construction, under the portico and in at the bronze doors. Inside the gate, Girolamo waits, holding the reins of Elia's palfrey. The two men exchange hurried remarks: Girolamo will follow the soldiers, Elia will take the shortest way, through streets hung with silks and strewn with branches where the citizens thought to honor their saint. Elia will be at the church in time to open the doors and stand ready to receive the treasure that is his. When the soldiers arrive, bearing the coffin, only six will pass through, then Elia alone will slide the bolt in place, barring the howling mob. A thousand tapers will flicker in the dark vaulted rooms, lighting the way down below the floor, down the makeshift steps to the crypt carved from solid rock, where he will direct the soldiers to lodge the coffin. He will send them away. He will slide the stones into place, sealing the tomb. The staircase will be pulled up, another layer of stone will hide the opening, the friars will fulminate, the Lord Pope will denounce Elia and lay sanctions against the Commune, but the crypt will not be found.

The basilica will be completed, the friars lodged in the *convento*. Elia will leave the friars to serve the emperor, whom some call the Antichrist, and with him will be excommunicated from the solace of the sacraments. For six hundred years, no one will solve the mystery. Francesco di Pietro Bernardone's bones will remain, as Brother Elia planned, unmolested, the jewel of the basilica, revered but unseen, like a string of invaluable pearls glistening miraculously in the darkness of the grave.

On His Illness

A Convalescent

Obedience subjects a man
to everyone on earth,
And not only to men,
but to all the beasts as well
and to the wild animals.
So that they can do what they like with him,
as far as God allows them.

—ST. FRANCIS OF ASSISI
The Praises of the Virtues

They hadn't known where else to take him. The doctors forbade the Portiuncula; it was a malarial swamp. Francesco had refused invitations to palaces and hermitages from every province, and he was postponing Cardinal Ugolino, who wanted him in Rieti where the pope's doctors could treat him. Only Sister Chiara's suggestion pleased him. They would build him a shelter near her convent where, from behind the safety of their grille, the nuns could supervise his care.

His care wasn't complicated. He wanted to lie on the floor in the dark. Indeed, there was no need even for a candle; he was entirely blind and so exhausted from preaching that he could walk only a few steps unaided. The brothers gathered reeds and sticks and threw up three walls which Brother Rufino patched with mud until the shelter looked like an enormous beehive growing out of the high stone wall of the convent. Inside it was sweltering, and the heavy cloth they hung over the doorway to keep out the mosquitoes made it hotter still. Pacifico and Rufino brought in a low table which they placed against the back wall; Leone borrowed a stool and a jug from Bishop Guido, who agreed grudgingly, as it was his opinion that Francesco should stay with him, where he could have proper nourishment. If he ate the poor stuff the sisters ate, the bishop complained, he would be dead in a week.

Chiara supplied a mat, and because he was so ill, she begged him to accept a pillow she had sewn and stuffed with goose feathers. He kept it one night, then sent it back to her with a warning that it was stuffed with devils, he had not slept one wink. Brother Angelo found a flat rock in the road which suited Francesco perfectly. He was not going to start sleeping on pillows.

He wanted to be left alone, especially at night, but he had been in his new refuge scarcely a week when the visitors began. He heard them scratching in the walls and in the thatch overhead, then he felt the first one rush across his legs. This hut was not to be a resting place, but a place of further trials. He heard one, then another, dropping from the low ceiling, scurrying frantically, though there was certainly no danger from him. One bumped into his bare feet, then, with small, sharp claws, pushed past him. He brushed away another burrowing in the folds of his tunic, which was a mistake, for the frightened creature rushed up his chest and into his beard. Francesco cried out into the darkness, but only the mice heard him. There were more and more of them. He sat up and waved his arms over his head. Tiny, swift claws raced up his spine like a chill, then he felt the soft brush of fur against his ear. He fell back upon his mat, pressing his lips together to keep in a shout. The darkness around him was astounding, as dense as lead, and the stifling heat drew streams of perspiration from every pore. He could feel it pooling in the hollows behind his clavicle and running off his brow into his ear. All he could hear was the sound of the nervous creatures, scratching and jumping, giving sudden, high-pitched cries. How busy they were, swarming over him. One was still, perched atop his left knee, another was tearing at the mat between his feet. They would eat the mat out from under him. "God be merciful to me, a sinner," he said softly. And there was his own voice in the darkness, as reassuring as the caress of an old friend. Louder this time, he sent up his petition. "God be merciful to me, a sinner." He threw up one hand to bat away the small, sinewy body that he sensed, falling from the thatch above his face.

In the morning, the friars come down from Assisi, down past the field of grain and through the olive grove, the old familiar path. Leone has half a loaf of bread, Angelo carries a leather tankard full of pig's-foot broth that Bishop Guido has pressed upon him.

Masseo has lashed a ceramic pitcher to his side with his waist cord. He will use it to carry water from the convent well. Already the sun is blazing, and the parched, cracked earth beneath their bare feet is hot. The air, dry and acrid, burns in their nostrils. In a voice as flat as the drone of the insects flitting over their shaggy heads, Rufino recites the morning antiphon and the others join in their turns, praising God routinely, for they are too tired and dispirited for anything more. The brotherhood, once the source of so much joy and pride to its founder, is in such disarray that all who care for him decline to speak of it. They keep the rumors from him. They do the bidding of Brother Elia, but they stick to the old Rule, begging their own bread while Elia is conversing with his cook on the best method of stewing pigeons. He is solicitous of Francesco's health, but is he not most anxious to know the exact moment when he will be able to drop the pretense of caring? These four, Masseo, Angelo, Leone, and Rufino, Francesco's companions in the early days when they were driven from the town by outraged shop-keepers, when they took shelter in the woods and lived like resourceful animals with spirits as high as the treetops, now are tired, middle-aged men, trudging along in the sultry morning air with hearts full of suspicion. They cross the bare patch of ground that borders the convent, then go single file between the cypress trees and the cool stone wall. Just ahead is the dark lump of the lean-to, jutting out from the smooth, pale stone like a black wart on a fair complexion. Leone arrives first at the doorway, but he does not go in. Instead, he looks back at his companions with a smile of surprising sweetness, surprising in a face as rough and coarse as his. He nods toward the door. They know why; they hear it too. Francesco has a strong, clear voice, and he is singing at full volume. They do not recognize the tune or the words: "For she is useful, humble, precious, and pure." They gather close, exchanging amused, indulgent looks. "Be praised, my Lord, for Brother Fire, by whom you light up the night, for he is fair and merry, mighty and strong."

So he is happy here, in the place they have made for him. Despite his illness, his blindness, the constant pain in his head, he is singing as cheerfully as a morning lark. Masseo steps forward and pushes the curtain aside. Light floods the hovel. He lets out a soft cry of dismay and backs away, holding the cloth so that the others looking past him can see what he has seen. Francesco lies upon his back, his arms folded over his chest, his hands partly hidden in his beard. His eyes are open, and though he cannot see, he appears to be looking right at them. He has not stopped singing; his beautiful voice pours out to them, framing the praises he has passed the night in composing. The mice are everywhere. They cover the floor, squirm into the cracks in the walls, leap frantically from the table, trying to escape the light. Two dive into the sleeves of the singer, one jumps from his chest to his forehead, then rushes out the door past the four horrified friars, who step gingerly out of its path. "Francesco," Angelo exclaims.

Francesco breaks off his singing and, with difficulty, raises himself onto his elbows. A mouse darts across his hand. "Angelo," he calls out cheerfully. "At last you are here. I want to send for Brother Pacifico at once. I have composed a wonderful new song and I want him to write it down for us all."

A Visit to the Doctor

Let each man glory in his own sufferings and not in another's.

—ST. FRANCIS OF ASSISI
Chronica Fratris Jordani

Cardinal Ugolino will be delayed no longer. He has been in Rieti for weeks, the Lord Pope's own physicians are in attendance, and he is certain they can relieve the torment of Brother Francesco's eye disease. His message invokes the vow of Holy Obedience—it is not a suggestion or an invitation. The four friars are to leave San Damiano at once.

They arrive at the city on a market day, having walked three days across the wide green valley, stopping at night to rest and to wash their sore feet, begging food from travelers they encounter on the road. Since Spoleto, these have been few, and they are weak with hunger. The narrow streets overflow with soldiers and merchants, clerks and clerics, servants and slaves, all in some way attached to the papal court, having come up from Rome with their master to escape the pitched battles in the streets. They upbraid one another in the rapid dialect of their city, which the friars, passing among them, grimace to hear. Brother Francesco keeps his eyes down. His face is concealed by the woven reed hat the brothers have made to protect his weeping eyes from the sun. He keeps his hands hidden in his sleeves; his feet are wrapped in woolen socks and protected by the leather slippers Sister Chiara has made for him, which slap against the stones and give him a queer, duck-footed gait. His three friends gather close around him, for he cannot see well enough to find his own way, and if he is recognized he will draw a crowd. The world is not indifferent to him now, but he is too ill to preach. The silent, anxious group makes its way, dodging the stamping horses, through the boisterous crowds, the clamorous barking of dogs, the cries of street vendors, past the wide portico of the cathedral, where two black friars, arguing about some fine point of faith, fail to notice them; along a narrow alley, where a family of cats drowses in the last rays of the sun, to the heavy bolted doors of the cardinal's residence. Here they give their names to the guards. At the words "Brother Francesco of Assisi," the two soldiers drop their hauteur and peer closely beneath the strange headgear at the downcast face of this famous personage, who stands quietly dabbing his eyes with the strip of rag he carries now wherever he goes. "Il Santo," they agree, and in the next moment, they throw open the heavy doors and usher the friars into the cardinal's reception room. A servant, occupied in lighting the vast array of candles ranged along the walls and in sconces on every available surface, is dispatched to inform the cardinal that his guests have arrived.

Soon, from within the palace, they hear coming toward them—evidently in conversation with someone who is not given the opportunity to respond—the familiar booming voice of the prelate. Francesco removes his hat and turns to face the doorway. He cannot see the cardinal, who appears now at the far end of the marble hall, nor the thin, rat-faced man, dressed oddly in a wide collar of white wool, an embroidered doublet, a scarlet cape, and pointed shoes, who trots along at the cardinal's side; but he knows, they all know, that this is the doctor, trained, equipped, and eager to try the fortitude of a saint.

Francesco is seated upon a bench in a low-ceilinged, mud-thatched room, his face bathed in the glow of the coals burning in a brazier near his feet. His companions stand near him, their eyes fixed upon the doctor, who crouches before the fire arranging his various irons upon the grate. He is dressed more soberly today, as befits the seriousness of the business, though his shoes are embroidered and absurdly pointed, and his short red doublet is glossy and so stiff it rustles as he rises to his feet, informing his patient that he will proceed with the operation when the irons are as white as the coals.

The friars had not stayed long at the cardinal's palace. Word of Francesco's arrival quickly spread through Rieti, and the populace showed no mercy. They crowded about the doors and windows and shouted his name. The boldest slipped past the guards and ran madly about, throwing open doors and snatching whatever they could find, bits of food they would claim he had tasted, a cushion he had surely sat upon, a napkin he must have pressed to his suppurating eyes. Ugolino was good-natured; it was only the people's faith, after all, that drove them to such excesses, but when one young ruffian was relieved of two of the cardinal's gold and coral spoons, even he agreed that the wisest course might be to follow Francesco's wishes and move him to the hermitage at Fonte Colombo, where the doctor could attend him without interference and the brothers would be available to care for him in his convalescence.

So they had brought him here, just as the sun was setting, disguised in a cloak the bishop provided. When he proved too weak to walk, Brother Masseo and Brother Bernardo joined their hands to make a kind of chair, and in this way they carried him, as they had when they brought him down from La Verna. He was subdued, terrified, as they all were, of the ordeal to come. Being branded by the doctor would be pain of a different order from that of his rapture on La Verna, where he had been branded by Christ. This time there would be no passion, no ecstasy, no consummation, only ordinary suffering at the hands of a man who had only suffering to offer. But if it would give him some relief from the agony of his eyes, he had admitted to the cardinal, he would endure it, and for the love of God, he would gladly endure it.

The doctor turns from his irons to examine once again the inflamed, weeping eyes of his patient. The doctors at San Damiano had applied poultices of feverfew and marjoram, which had drawn down quantities of pus, as if they had opened a floodgate. This treatment was, the doctor explained, exactly wrong for such a disease. These were butchers, not doctors, and the famous Brother Francesco was lucky they had not killed him. The proper course was obvious: as the vessels exuded pus, they must be sealed, not irritated and drawn. The doctor has seen and cured many such cases and has no doubt that in a few weeks his patient will be singing not God's praises but his own, all over the countryside.

The coals begin to crumble and the embers hiss. Francesco bends toward the brazier until he can feel the heat on his forehead. "My brother Fire," he says. "Be courteous to me at this hour, because I loved you formerly and still love you, for the love of the Lord, who created you." The doctor, rolling back his sleeves, eyes his patient doubtfully. Francesco, absorbed in his address, continues, "I beseech our Creator who made you to temper your heat now so that I may be able to bear it." At these last words, he raises his eyes to the brothers huddled behind the doctor. He has calmed his own fear, but panic grips their hearts, and as the doctor lifts the first iron, one by one they slip from the room. The silence that follows as they gather outside the door is more unnerving than a cry of pain. A nauseating smell of burning flesh floods from the narrow chamber, filling their mouths and nostrils so that they clap their hands over their faces. Brother Rufino drops to his knees, then swoons flat onto the hard earth floor. Brother Leone sobs openly, calling on Christ to grant their holy father's humble petition. The smell grows more intense; they cannot catch a breath without swallowing it, so they flail helplessly, gasping the poisonous air.

In the room, the doctor lays the iron back upon the grate and turns to examine his handiwork. Francesco does not move, he has not moved, has not spoken, clenched his fists, cried out, or wept. He gazes placidly into the middle air with the vacant, listening attitude of the blind. The bright red flesh between his ear and eye-brow still sizzles, and at the edges of the wound thin strips curl away, blackened by the heat of the iron. Carefully, the doctor bends over him and removes a few hairs from the singed brow. "Now for the other side," he says.

Brother Body Wins the Day

Brother Body is our cell, and our soul is the hermit.

—ST. FRANCIS OF ASSISI
Scripta Leonis

Leone slaps his forehead with the heel of his hand, and Rufino shrugs. The doctor regards them, impervious to their protests. The patient must take the medicine, he insists, and it is not his business to persuade him to do it. "It will ease the pain, he will sleep." He holds out to them the vial in its leather case. "It is bitter," he says. "You must dilute it in wine, or in honey." Leone takes the medicine, lifts the stopper, and sniffs.

"He won't listen to reason," Rufino says.

"Tell him to listen to his body."

Leone smiles. "He calls his body Brother Ass."

"We could tell him that as surely as God sent his pain, he has sent this medicine," Rufino suggests.

"Elia has already tried that," Leone replies.

The doctor has no more patience. The calls on his science are numerous; there are cardinals and even kings who do not spurn the relief he provides. He rises from the rickety bench provided by the friars and looks around the chilly cell without interest. "Tell him the Lord Pope has sent his command that he is to take this medicine," he says, and, pulling his cloak over his shoulders, stoops to avoid hitting his head on the lintel as he passes through the door. The friars sit quietly in the darkening room, regarding the medicine, which Leone has set on the floor between them.

"He finds the new brother from Padova most gracious in his speech," Leone offers.

"It's worth a try," Rufino agrees.

. . .

58

The novice arrives at the cell of Father Francesco, his eyes bright, his manner urgent and full of confidence. Francesco has confided to Leone that this youth reminds him of himself when he first came to the knowledge that he would not be alone in his passion to renounce the world and serve Lady Poverty, that her pure beauty would attract a host of followers until the end of the world. Leone greets the youth at the door, stepping outside to have a word before admitting him to the presence of the dying man. "He is in great pain," Leone explains. "He knows that you have been summoned to persuade him to accept the medicine the doctor has prepared for him."

"How am I to do it?" the young man complains.

"If it is to be done?" Leone says. "That will be up to the Holy Spirit."

The novice smiles broadly at this, and Leone sees in that smile some trace of the delight in life that once animated the face of his dying friend. Even now, as Francesco lies in an agony of suffering—unable even to sit up without assistance, vomiting most of what he eats, sleepless, wracked by headaches, blind, often confused in his thinking—he still speaks sometimes in the old way, responding to a chance remark with the lively wit that has brought so many fools to wisdom and the powerful of the world to humility. "We will go in," Leone says, opening the door and ushering the young man inside.

The room is dark, the only window covered with a canvas cloth. Francesco cannot tell whether it is day or night, but his caretakers are so accustomed to protecting his eyes that they continue the practice out of habit. "The Lord grant you peace," the novice says to the shadowy body stretched upon a bed of planks near the door.

"This is our new brother from Padova," Francesco says hoarsely.

Leone presses the youth forward. "He has come to counsel you."

"God knows I need wise counsel," the invalid responds, waving one hand out toward the novice, who takes it quickly in his own, hiding his astonishment at its resemblance to the bandaged talon of some wounded hawk, like the one people say befriended the blessed Francesco on Mount La Verna, attending his cell for matins and vespers.

"I will speak if God will guide my tongue," the young man says.

The claw grips him more tightly as Francesco pulls himself closer. The effort produces a muffled cry, as a wounded doe moans when she staggers in the forest, death's arrow lodged in her bleeding breast. Leone steps forward to help the holy father, lifting him easily so that he rests upon one side. His face is now bathed in the dim light from the window, and the brother can see the flaked skin on his lips, the sunken, sightless eyes, the nose which juts out sharply, refined to bone by his illness.

"My dearest son," Francesco says. "What do you think of the fact that my conscience murmurs so frequently about the care of my body? It is afraid I will indulge it too much in its illness and be anxious to come to its aid by means of delicacies carefully sought after. Not that it can take delight anymore in anything after it has been worn down so long by illness, and after all urge to satisfy taste has left it." He releases the novice's hand and folds his own over his chest.

"Tell me," the brother replies, "if you will, Father, with how much diligence your body obeyed your commands when it could."

Leone's eyebrows lift, and he presses his lips together. He backs away from the interview, seating himself on a flat rock that serves as both table and chair. Francesco is silent for a moment, then replies. "I bear witness concerning it, son, that it was obedient in all things; it spared itself in nothing, but rushed almost headlong to obey all my commands. It shirked no labor, it refused no discomfort, so long as it could do what was commanded. In this

I and it agreed perfectly that we would serve the Lord Christ without any reluctance."

The novice frowns at this response, though it has provided him with his argument. "Where then, Father, is your generosity, where are your kindness and discretion? Is this a worthy way to repay faithful friends, to accept a kindness willingly, but when the giver is in need not to repay him as he deserves? What would you have done up till now in the service of Christ your Lord without the help of your body? Has it not, as you said, exposed itself to every danger on this account?"

Francesco nods his head slowly, his forefinger stroking his beard flat against his chin. "I confess, my son," he says, "that this is very true."

The novice casts a triumphant glance at Leone but does not catch his eye. He turns back to Francesco. His excitement at the irresistible charge of his argument animates his features, and his voice takes on gravity, as if he is addressing a crowd. "Is this reasonable, then, that you abandon so faithful a friend in such great need, a friend who has exposed himself and all that is his for you even unto death? Far be it from you, Father, help and staff of the afflicted, far be it from you this sin against the Lord."

Francesco does not stir. His eyes are closed. For one moment, the novice fears he has gone beyond all need of remedy or reason, but then his lips move, and he says softly, "Bless you, my son." He rolls onto his back, his eyes fly open, and he cries out joyfully, "Rejoice, Brother Body, and forgive me, for, behold, I now give heed to your complaints."

The novice opens his palms to the air and turns to Brother Leone, who has poured the contents of the vial into a wooden bowl and is struggling with the lid of a honey jar. Leone looks up, smiling broadly, though his eyes are damp with tears. "Well done, Brother," he says.

On the Stigmata

A Mountain Storm

Our lexicon associates visions with mysticism, irrationality, occultism, impracticality and madness. From our point of view the visionary is a person who sees what isn't there; his visions separate him from reality. In the middle ages, visions defined reality.

—CARROLY ERICKSON
The Medieval Vision

Every day Francesco goes farther from the shelter and closer to the edge. When Leone brings the food and water, he sees him there, perched on the rocky ledge, his arms outstretched at his sides, his face lifted toward the intense blue of the sky. Leone wants to speak, to warn him back, but he has promised not to, so he leaves the bread and water on the rocky outcropping near the shelter and goes back down, filled with anxiety, to the others. To get there he has to cross the flimsy log bridge they have made, which terrifies him, for if he slips and falls into the chasm below, he does not doubt that he will shatter on the rocks like a clay jug. He goes on hands and knees, clutching the log and praying every inch of the way. Then he scrambles along the downhill path, clinging to bushes and tender saplings that bend one to another, handing him safely down over the treacherous decline like sympathetic friends. As he hurries across the clearing where they have made their huts, Masseo and Angelo come out to meet him. They sit together on the ground in the shade of an enormous beech. Masseo shares out the fresh loaf the soldiers brought that morning. There are beans and a cabbage as well; the count is too generous.

"Did you see him?" Angelo asks.

Leone nods, chewing his bread. He is uncertain whether to voice his fears. They are supposed to be meditating upon Christ's suffering in the garden: deserted by his friends, branded a criminal, certain of betrayal. "He is weeping," he says when he has swallowed his bread.

Masseo and Angelo exchange guarded looks.

They came to this mountain in high spirits. Francesco had

accepted Count Orlando's offer without his usual reservations about the hospitality of the wealthy and powerful. The wise count had not offered them a seat at his table, soft beds, or polished floors; he did not seek, as so many did, to make house pets of the friars. Rather, he offered them a rugged wilderness in which to pray and fast, a place uninhabited because inhospitable. Francesco was convinced the invitation was from God.

The plan was simple. The friars would walk for four days to La Verna, build their usual huts, and make a lent over the forty days between the Assumption and the feast of St. Michael the Archangel. Francesco's sight was failing, but he was determined to go on as if it made no difference. He held his hands out before him, stumbling in the road between Masseo and Leone, singing the *Laudes* in his strong voice. But early on the second day, he fell to his knees in the road and admitted that he would accept the services of a donkey if some farmer could be found to make the loan. Angelo and Masseo went ahead, leaving Francesco and Leone in the shade of a bay tree. Leone could see their destination, the gray mountain of La Verna rising sharply from the green floor of the valley, the peak partially obscured in a cloud, pierced through and held in place by a dark green swath of pines. It would be cooler there.

The farmer Angelo and Masseo found was a querulous fellow who never stopped talking and complaining. They piled Francesco onto his donkey and continued on the road, but there was no more singing, only the repetitive drone of this tiresome man. The donkey trudged along, hanging his head sleepily, his big ears lowered as if to close out the sound of his master's nagging. The man upbraided the world, from the emperor to the crows which rose up like black waves over the dry fields as they passed. At length he shouted up to Francesco, who rocked about miserably on the creature's uncomfortable spine, "Are you really that Brother Francesco everyone is talking about?"

Francesco smiled down upon him, clutching a few strands of the short matted mane to steady himself. "Yes," he replied.

"I want to give you some advice," the man continued. "And that is to be as good as people say you are."

"Stop a moment," Francesco called out. Masseo turned in his tracks, grasped the donkey's halter, and brought the procession to an abrupt halt. Francesco clambered down to the dusty road and got to his knees before the farmer. Then, to the astonishment of the rustic and the amusement of the brothers, he bent over the fellow's dung-encrusted clogs and kissed them repeatedly, thanking him for this valuable and welcome admonition. The man stood with his mouth open, his sweating brow furrowed with concern, so thoroughly confused that for several moments he could find nothing to say.

This was in the old spirit, and when the farmer insisted on helping Francesco back onto the donkey, the brothers gathered around, offering encouragement and praise. They had not gone far before the farmer reverted to his litany of grievances, but his heart was no longer in it; he hesitated, digressed, and even imagined excuses for his enemies. Francesco had disarmed him, and they were once again the cheerful friars who would save the world by example.

But after they arrived at the mountain, and Count Orlando came out with his soldiers to welcome them, Francesco's mood darkened. The first night they stayed together, exhausted from the long trip and content to sleep peacefully in the huts the soldiers had helped them put up near a beech tree. At dawn Francesco wandered off, as was his habit, in search of some secluded place to pray. He did not appear again until sext and then stayed only long enough to receive communion from Leone. He hardly spoke, appearing, they agreed, distracted. He kept his head tilted toward the forest, as if he was listening to someone talking there in the shadows just beyond the clearing. He refused the food they offered him and cautioned them against the count's hospitality. "The more we cling to Lady Poverty," he advised, "the more will we be honored." Then he went back, touching the trunks of the trees as he passed, pausing once to stare at a rock, then stepping gingerly around it, back into the forest.

The time passed. The days grew cooler, shorter; the nights were black. Francesco wanted a new shelter in a place he had found, high up, near a cliff where the view on a clear day drew the eye across green valleys and low hills all the way to the sea. He could not see it, but he liked the exposure of the place, the way the rock thrust into a void, so that he seemed to be standing alone in the sky. He would stay there for the rest of their Lent.

Something was going to happen, he explained. He didn't know what. He would see no one, talk to no one; only Leone was to come twice a day, to bring him a little food and sing matins. The feast of the Exaltation of the Cross was near; he wanted to contemplate nothing but Christ's passion; he wished to enter into it here, they must all enter into it, each in his own way, as they had never done before. He prayed to experience himself the physical agony of the Crucifixion as well as the full redeeming force and intensity of the love through which that suffering was so willingly embraced, that passion in which joy and sadness, pain and ecstasy were inextricably commingled.

They did, as they always did, what he asked. When they had finished the shelter, they left him there, and Leone crawled across the log twice a day.

"Did he eat anything?" Angelo asks.

"No," Leone replies.

Francesco stands alone on the bare ledge, his arms outstretched, his palms turned up, his head dropped forward so that his chin nearly touches his breastbone. The muscles in his arms vibrate, protesting the strain of this unnatural position, but he is not listening to his arms. His lips move ceaselessly, forming rote words, but no sound comes out. His eyes are closed.

Before him, jutting up and out like the prow of a ship, is a narrow raised slab of stone. The sun has set, the valley far below has faded from green to gray, but it is not yet night. A bank of ominous clouds is poised before the mountainside, gathering force. Francesco doesn't need to see to know a storm is approaching. He can feel the cool caress of the freighted air on his face and neck, he can smell and taste the moisture in it and hear the urgent breeze whispering through the grass tufts lodged in the rocks near his feet. Like the grasses, he is rooted and patient, a frail figure in his rags and length of rope, his bare toes splayed against the stones. There is nothing tenuous about him; he will not move.

A drop strikes his brow, another smashes against his palm, sharp and cold. Behind him, from the branches of a stunted laurel, a piercing cry issues, then he hears the beating of wings as a hawk hurtles past him over the edge and up into the brooding mass of the clouds. He lifts his head and opens his eyes—the hawk has startled him—but he makes no more movement than this. He can feel rather than see the big wings snap in, then spread wide, as the creature catches a powerful updraft and disappears into the dark center of the storm, where Francesco is trying hard to send his own soul. "Who are you?" he asks.

More drops answer him. His lips are moistened, his burning eyes are bathed, icy water soaks his beard and slips down his neck in a thin stream. He has lost all feeling in his arms. A sudden gust whirls around him, pressing the damp wool of his tunic against his legs and chest. He closes his eyes and listens. The wind hisses like angry voices whispering, but beyond it he can hear other sounds; the world is far from quiet. Small animals, rabbits, chipmunks, and lizards scurry among the stones and in the undergrowth of scrubby bushes, searching for shelter. The trees creak and groan, and their branches scrape together, making a hollow rattling sound like a skeleton getting up from a long sleep. The raindrops spatter against the hard ground, more and more of them, and he hears each separate small explosion, as if a great mocking crowd stood all around him, tapping their tongues against their teeth repeatedly, making no effort at words.

If the world mocks him, if even his own brothers have no use for him, doesn't their contempt only kindle the flame of his love for them?

It is dark now, there is no light from the sun, moon, or stars, nothing but a great blackness pouring down a cold torrent like a rain of arrows from the bows of a million archers. There are as many drops as there are stars, it is as if the stars have turned to drops and the wind gathers them and flings them against him in sheets. "Who am I?" he asks, but he can't hear his own voice, and cold water fills his mouth so that he is forced to swallow. He stares up into the blackness. As far as he can tell, his arms have frozen into place; nor can he feel his feet which are down there, some-where, in the icy pools that have gathered among the rocks. He sways with the force of the wind, but otherwise does not move.

In the camp below him, the four friars struggle to hold their shelters together, but the branches fly off in every direction, and the vines girding the walls snap like bits of thread. A section of mud-daubed wall collapses on Brother Angelo, and his compan-ions rush to pull him out. They shout to one another over the storm. Angelo is not hurt, only God has told him to lie down for a moment. They are laughing and shouting as they rush into the woods, clinging to the trees to keep from falling.

In the morning, in the still, bright air that follows the storm, Leone will find Francesco seated on the rock outside his shelter, wet, shivering, absorbed in wrapping a few strips of wool he has torn from his breeches around the wounds in his bleeding feet.

What Is an Eye

*Chaste embraces, gentle feelings, a holy kiss, pleasing
conversation, modest laughter, joyous looks, a single eye,
a submissive spirit, a peaceable tongue, a mild answer,
oneness of purpose, ready obedience, unwearied hand,
all these were found in them.*

—THOMAS OF CELANO
The First Life of St. Francis

At dinner, Brother Angelo told how they came down from La Verna where they had made a lent, and where Father Francesco bid them all to enter with full hearts the awful passion of the Savior. They had all heard the story of how Brother Leone saw the holy father, his arms outstretched, his eyes bathed in tears, standing in the air high above the earth, lost in his meditations. When they left that place, Angelo said, Father Francesco had bid them stop so that he might say farewell to this mountain, which, because of the blessing visited upon him there, would be forever a sacred and holy retreat.

But what blessing could this be? the novice asks himself as he hurries along the leaf-strewn path that leads to Brother Francesco's cell. The days are still warm, but now, at night, his bare feet are chilled as if they have been plunged into an icy stream, as cold as that holy fountain which sprang from the rock at Mount La Verna when the farmer complained of thirst, and Father Francesco struck the rock with his stick and called forth a spring. How could Father Francesco have been blessed on that mountain when he has come back so ill his closest companions speak of him in whispers? The novice rushes through the darkness, clutching a skin of chamois leather, as white as cream and softer than the breath of angels, which Brother Illuminato has given him to take to Brother Leone, who does not ever leave the holy father's side. Once he is inside the father's cell, the novice promises himself, he will keep his eyes open and his wits about him, so that he may see for himself if the rumors are true, that Father Francesco bears the wounds of the Crucifixion on his own flesh. Many miracles have been worked by this holy man, but now God has worked a miracle upon him: this is what the friars say, and in the towns, people say Father Francesco is the second Christ and that with his death the earth will crack open, the dead will rise up to be judged, and the world will come to an end.

In the clearing ahead, the light from the cell flickers, then pours out in a sudden slash as Brother Leone opens the door and peers into the night. So as not to startle his brother, the novice calls out, *"Pax et bonum,"* the greeting God gave Father Francesco long ago, before he gave him brothers, when his neighbors called him mad and his own father cursed him in the streets.

"Pax et bonum," Leone replies, but without enthusiasm. Brother Leone is more beloved by Father Francesco than any of the brothers, even Brother Elia, whom he has entrusted with the entire order, but Brother Leone he has entrusted with something more precious—the care of his own body—and that burden has in these last days taken all the joy from Brother Leone's eyes: his speech is terse, though never unkind.

"Brother Illuminato has bid me bring this skin to you," the novice begins, moving rapidly out of the darkness and into the warm influence of the light. He longs to have Brother Leone confide in him; to hear the sorrows that have left him weary and silent. Leone takes the chamois and runs his fingers over the smooth folds. The novice looks past him into the room, and there, seated on the edge of his bed, which is just a plank set into the wattled wall, is Father Francesco, wearing only a hair shirt and ragged breeches. His head is dropped forward so that his beard touches his chest. The light from the lamp flickers over him, making mysterious puddles of shadow on his cheeks, his lips, and his feet. His feet, the novice observes with a shock of delight—for here surely is proof of the rumors that circulate in the Portiuncula, like flies lighting and rising and lighting again upon a corpse—Brother Francesco's feet are covered in woolen socks.

Brother Leone turns away, taking the skin to a table on which the novice sees a morsel of dark bread, a jug, a knife, and the lamp, which sends a thin plume of smoke to the ceiling. "This will do very well," Leone says, examining the skin in the light of the lamp. The novice, quivering with curiosity, takes the opportunity to step inside. Father Francesco does not lift his head or greet the novice. The friars say he is nearly blind now and that he cannot bear the light of day. When he goes out, his eyes are bandaged, and Brother Leone leads him like a child.

"*Pax et bonum,* Father," the novice says, his voice seeming to him too loud, too full of vivacity in this dim sickroom.

Father Francesco lifts his head, though not his eyes, and says into the cool air before his face, "*Pax et bonum.*" How the novice thrills at that voice, which is, as they say, light and fresh, like water rushing in a brook.

"I am Brother Girolando of Gubbio, and I have brought you a fine skin which Brother Illuminato sends to you with his warm salutations."

"Illuminato," Father Francesco says, as if the name gives him pleasure to say it, as if to say it is to summon Illuminato into his presence.

Brother Leone turns from the table where he has spread out the skin. "Illuminato has been praying incessantly for the count, who has given him this skin."

"He must pray harder," Francesco observes.

"He has written a note, thanking him for sending us the wrong skin," Leone replies.

The novice looks from Brother Leone to Father Francesco and back again. He wants desperately to enter this camaraderie with some light witticism that will spark their interest, but his mind is blank. The atmosphere in the room is rarefied, and he shivers as a cool ribbon of air passing in from the window wraps once around his neck. Brother Leone leaves the table and takes up a dark bundle from the corner, which he holds out to the novice. "Take this to whomever is doing the washing."

"That is Brother Giovanni," the novice says, holding out his arms. When he receives the bundle, a strong odor rises from it, and he pulls his face away with a grimace. Brother Leone stands watching him, a thin smile all that gives evidence of his feelings. The novice lifts a fold of the cloth; it is a robe, and one side of it is damp with dark blood.

He can neither move nor speak, and his heart thuds in his chest. They have handed him the proof. He has been chosen by Father Francesco to carry the bloodstained robe forth so that all may know Father Francesco has been wounded by an angel who was surely the Lord Christ himself. He will go to Brother Stefano, who entered the order with him, both in hopes of seeing this holy man before his death, which all agree can not be far away, and discuss with him the best way to make public the revelation of the robe. Father Francesco turns his blind eyes toward the novice, and though his gaze is empty and abstract, the young friar feels it probing him tenderly, as a mother touches her sick child, searching out the locus of pain. The novice looks to Brother Leone, who only smiles at him, waiting for the question they both know is forming in his head. He holds the bundle out gingerly, lifting the damp fold. "Whose blood is this?" he asks.

Leone's eyes flicker to the holy man, and the novice's gaze follows. Francesco is sitting up stiffly now, his thin legs dangling over the edge of the bed, his attention entirely concentrated on the novice, who receives it with entirely feigned calm. Now the confidence he longs for will surely be his; the father will ask his son to guard the miraculous truth, or he will tell him how and to whom it is to be revealed. And he will obey, he will do as he is directed, even if it means he cannot tell Brother Stefano the news of his special selection.

Father Francesco raises his hand, pointing his index finger at the corner of his bleary eye. "Ask what this is," he says, "if you don't know it is an eye."

Brother Leone chuckles softly, turning to the novice with a nod of dismissal. In a moment he is back on the hard ground outside, the door closed firmly behind him. He clutches the robe to his chest and breathes in the confounding perfume of the founder's mysterious blood. The path is ahead of him, his mission is simple and direct, yet he trembles as he makes his way, and he understands at last that his vanity is all that stands between him and the everpresent, overpowering love of God.

Brother Leone Is Transported

Charity seeks not her own; but the solitary life removed from all others has only one aim, that of serving the ends of the individual concerned . . . if you live alone, whose feet will you wash?

—ST. BASIL
The Ascetical Works of St. Basil

The shadows have lengthened, and the night birds have begun their plaintive chorus. Leone lights the lamp, adjusts the flame, and returns to his occupation, cutting out long strips from a square of white wool. Francesco sits next to him on the stone, his hands resting palm-up in his lap. Leone's method is to cut the edge and then rip the strips away. The repeated complaint of the tearing cloth is the only sound in the dim cell. Francesco dabs briefly at his eye with the sleeve of his robe.

It is always worse on Saturday because Francesco refuses to have the bandages changed on Friday, the day when the Lord Christ suffered on the cross. Leone has removed the cloths from Francesco's hands and feet without much difficulty, but they both know the wound in his side is the most painful to clean, as it bleeds more copiously than the others. So they leave it for last. Leone lays out his strips, takes up one, and kneels at Francesco's feet. Because the nail head protrudes from the flesh, he lays the strip beneath it, passing the cloth around the foot until it is level with the hard black disk. He does this carefully, gently. Moving the nail is excruciating to Francesco, though he never complains, only draws his breath in sharply. Leone reaches for another strip which he wraps around the first, then, cradling the foot in his hands, he slips on one of the wool socks the Poor Ladies have knitted for him. As he reaches for a strip to begin the other foot, he looks up at Francesco. His features are composed, and his eyes rest, or seem to rest, on Leone's mouth. "Bless you, brother lamb of God," he says. Leone smiles, pulls the cloth to him, and kneels again at Francesco's feet. They hear the sharp cries of ravens arriving at their night posts in the ilex trees outside the cell. The air has grown perceptibly cooler; a breeze stirs the bits of wool on the stone table.

When he has finished Francesco's feet and hands, Leone helps him pull his tunic over his head in order to change the wide bandage that wraps his torso. Francesco groans as he lifts his arms, and Leone winces, apologizing for the pain. Francesco's fingers flutter about the waist of his breeches, touching the edge of the bandage. Leone bends over to inspect it. The blood has soaked through and dried.

Leone has confessed to Brother Rufino the anxiety in his heart when he thinks of his own sinful nature and how unworthy he is to serve so holy a man, yet he is convinced that only through the grace of Father Francesco has his poor soul any hope of salvation. God has chosen Francesco as his instrument to save many souls, which would otherwise be damned, and Leone's most fervent prayer is that, through no merit of his own, but by his devotion to Francesco, he will be one of that select company of the redeemed. Yet, even as he nourishes that hope, he knows that he has no right to it, because he is so sinful and plagued by temptations.

Now, as he studies the bloodstained bandage, he feels a welling-up of emotions: fear, pity, devotion, heart-smiting love. For a moment he does not move, and Francesco asks, "What is it, brother lamb of Christ?"

Leone shivers, drawing away. "It's dry," he says, "but when I unwrap it, it will open again."

Francesco straightens his spine and opens his arms out from his sides as if praying, and perhaps he is. Leone unfastens the end of the bandage and slowly pulls away the outer layer. It comes loose easily, but with the next layer, he feels a slight resistance, and Francesco's knitted brow tells him what he already knows. "Forgive me, Father," Leone says, pulling the cloth free with a quick jerk. Francesco bites his lower lip without speaking. There is one layer to go, and it will be the most painful. Leone brings the loose part of the bandage just to the edge of the wound, then pulls it lightly to find the deepest part. Francesco's face has gone white, but he does not flinch. Instead, he raises one hand and lays it upon Leone's chest, just over his heart. "My dear son," he says softly.

Leone looks down at the bandaged hand pressing gently against his chest. The wonder of the moment overcomes him. Francesco's hand is like a burning sword plunged into his heart, inflaming him with such passionate devotion that his vision blurs and he gasps for air. How is it possible that he is here, tending the miraculous wounds of this new Christ, who is also his dearest friend and companion, his brother, father, mother, who inspired him when they were both young and in love with Lady Poverty to follow him on a great adventure of the soul? They have walked a thousand miles in this quest, only to come to this cell where Francesco touches Leone's heart with the hand which bears the proof that he is the most dearly loved of all those who serve the Lord Christ, because of all the saints, only he has been chosen to share in Christ's own suffering. "Francesco," Leone says, leaning into the hand that presses, that holds his heart, and meeting his beloved's eyes, which, though they can scarcely see him, still pour over him, like warm rain, forgiveness, love, perfect understanding. Brother Leone is swooning. He fears he will be destroyed by the power of this love. Yet his hands are still engaged in their task. With a cry of terror, commingled with joy, he pulls sharply at the cloth, freeing it from the wounded flesh. As he loses consciousness, he sees the blood gushing forth, and it seems to him that his whole body and soul are bathed and refreshed in this blood, which is shed for him, and which he cannot deserve.

On His Teaching

Wild Men and an Emperor

Therefore in A.D. 800, when the Empire was revived in the West under Charles the Great, it had already a serious political rival in the Papacy; and upon this rivalry all subsequent political thought of the Middle Ages is more or less definitely hinged. . . . It was assumed that Church and State were as inseparable as soul and body, yet needing no less careful and constant readjustment.

—G. G. COULTON
The Medieval Scene

A hunter from Foligno, inspecting his snares in the forest near Rivo Torto, saw two of them, dressed alike, their hair and beards unkempt; they approached him with the greeting "God give you peace," which was how he knew they were the Poor Men of Assisi. They told him they had gone begging in the town, that they had been turned away everywhere and come back empty-handed. When they left him, they walked into the forest, toward the stream; so, the man reasoned, that must be where they are living. This man heard also that two peasant women, stopping to cool their hands and faces in the stream, were frightened by wild men running among the trees. These men, they claim, were so decked with leaves and twigs they were as living trees. One of the women maintains she saw leafy branches growing from their sleeves where hands should have been.

A farmer who owns the land adjoining this wood was gathering chestnuts, when, he told his neighbor, he saw smoke billowing from the door of an abandoned shed which he had once used to stable two goats. He heard singing, beautiful singing in parts, such as one hears in church, pouring out of the door with the smoke. A miller from Foligno also passed this shack and spoke with one who was cooking beans in a pot outside the door. The miller was impressed by this man's simplicity and offered him a coin, but the man refused, saying he would take grain if the miller had any to spare, but he could not accept the coin because Francesco had forbidden the brothers to touch money.

So they have stopped there, having come from Roma with the pope's approval to live by a holy rule of Francesco's making, and they go out in twos begging and preaching up and down the roads between Foligno and Assisi. An old man from Spello has joined them, and an idiot from Le Marche. Anyone who wants to live according to the Gospel and give everything he owns to the poor may go there and be welcome, though the little shack is so crowded the Poor Men sleep sitting up. They dress in the poorest stuff and wear no shoes, but they are cheerful, living like animals, eating whatever they can find, and when it is dry out, they sleep on the bare ground with only the falling leaves to cover them.

But winter is at hand. Will they still be cheerful when the snows begin to fall?

On his journey from his northern fiefs to Roma—where he will be anointed by the Lord Pope Innocent—the new emperor, escorted by his knights and courtly retinue, has stopped at the gates of Assisi to receive the homage of the bishop and the podesta. The first standard-bearers of his cortege are already in view; far down the road, their bright banners flutter in the cool breeze. The procession is slow and stately, as befits the puissance of the emperor. The friars take turns running up and down the hill to monitor the steady progress, returning to the shelter where the others wait impatiently for the latest report.

Francesco is vexed by his companions' interest in this event. They want to go and stand in the road, gaping like children at the spectacle. One will feast his eyes on the horses, another will delight in the gold work on the bridles and saddles, another will exclaim upon the ranks of infantry, counting every pike and quarrel, another will memorize the fantastical figures emblazoned on every shield and name the noble houses he thereby recognizes, another will swear that the emperor looked right at him and nodded his head approvingly. Francesco has put them all under a vow of obedience; before the procession passes, they are to return to the shed and take their places behind the closed door, where they will recite the *Miserere,* all but Brother Bernardo, who will go to the road, find a hiding place behind some bush or tree, and shout out as the emperor goes by, "Your glory cannot last!" In this way, the world and the emperor will hear of the Poor Men who live without earthly glory and do not admire or ape the ways of the powerful. It has come to Francesco—God has told him in a dream—that this emperor will not live long and will die amid his riches weeping for his sins, which are beyond number.

Brothers Filippo and Masseo arrive from the road, breathing hard, wide-eyed with excitement. The first horses have passed, and such glorious knights have never been seen. Over their armor they wear long capes that cover their horses' backs to the tails, and these capes are black silk, lined in sable, as black as the night sky and brocaded all over in silver points like stars, and their gauntlets are inlaid with jet stones, and the mail on their arms is trimmed in gold. Francesco claps his hands over his ears; he does not intend to hear one more word about the emperor's parade. Brother Bernardo is to go at once and carry out his mission. As the friars stumble inside their shed, bumping into one another, they take their regular places, each beneath his own name, which Francesco has carved into the roof beams. They can hear the drums of the emperor's escort pounding in time with the marching feet of the foot soldiers. Francesco shoves Bernardo out the door. Then he drops the bar, leans against it as if he expects it to blow open, and begins the psalm, *"Miserere mei, Deus, secundum magnam misericordiam tuam . . ."*

Bernardo hurries along the path, his bare feet kicking up the carpet of yellow leaves that have lately fallen. Through the bare branches of the trees, he can see the white legs of the horses, the black steel of the riders' helmets, and flashes of bright blue or red in their banners and shields. His lips move silently, working over his message, summoning the courage to deliver it. He lurches into the open road, nearly colliding with a foot soldier who does not so much as glance at him as he shifts his shield to send him sprawling on the road. There, for a moment, Bernardo lies, gazing up at the underbelly of a horse. As he watches, the horse lifts his tail and lets fall a steaming clod of dung. He laughs. Surely this is the proper angle from which to view the emperor, but if he doesn't move quickly, he is liable to be trampled, so he rolls into the ditch and clambers to his feet. The parade moves past him, churning as relentlessly as a mill, only this one grinds out not flour but death. Weighted down with battle-axes, clubs, and swords, the foot soldiers wear odd, pointed basinets in the German style, with leather straps that fit so tightly beneath the chin they must prevent speech. A contingent of *pavesari* comes behind; only their heads and feet are visible behind the tall shields they carry before them, so they resemble a moving wall of jointed steel.

Bernardo looks about for a post from which to carry out his own battle order, but no camouflage presents itself. The road is wide, the ditch on either side bare and dusty, and if he calls out from the edge of the wood, he won't be heard over the pounding drums, the tramp of feet and hooves. After the *pavesari* comes a rank of mounted knights, their faces hidden in full helmets; then a company of noble lords and barons, attired not for battle but for display, their horses draped to the knees in heavy brocades with the escutcheon of their families worked into the pattern; their banners bear the heraldic lions, griffins, ravens, and bears. The high collars of their cloaks cover half their faces, their stiff domed hats are trimmed in furs and jewels. Many are fair-haired, square-jawed, blue-eyed, but there are a few swarthy, black-eyed Magyars on their small, sturdy mounts, draped in skins instead of silks, wearing cuirasses of tooled leather, their stiff, straight black hair jutting out from beneath leather caps lined in wolf fur.

Bernardo has spied a low knoll across the road, the perfect perch from which to sing his benediction. He dives into the procession, dodges a drummer who ignores him, runs afoul of one of the Magyars who casts him a baleful look and clips him hard on the ear with his leather buckler. The friar scrambles up the knoll, clutching his head between his hands, but he forgets the pain as he looks down the road, for there, just ahead, astride the biggest, blackest horse he has ever seen, draped from neck to knee in ermine, sable, and red silk embroidered in spun gold, is the emperor. His boots and stockings are red, even his gloves are red, studded with pearls. His head is bent beneath the weight of an enameled crown, topped by a cross of solid gold. The brim is so encrusted with faceted jewels that it envelops his face in a nimbus of white light.

The moment has arrived; the friar is equal to it. "Most high Lord Otto of Brunswick," Bernardo shouts, but no one hears him, indeed he hardly hears himself over the din of drums, boots, hooves, the metallic creaking of armor. He waves his arms and cries out with all his strength. "Your glory will not last!" A passing foot soldier turns his head to stare, then looks quickly away. Bernardo drops his arms, perplexed but determined. Francesco wants his message delivered, not to the air but to the emperor.

This emperor is very close now, rocking back and forth sleepily on the wide back of his great warhorse. His bejeweled fingers rest loosely on the ivory pommel of his saddle. He has been passing through the countryside for weeks. Sometimes there are shouting, enthusiastic crowds, sometimes he is admired only by the blank faces of sunflowers or the lazily genuflecting fields of grain. He raises his eyes now and then to take in some particular face or an interesting feature of the landscape, or to exchange a comment with one of his barons. He does not see the shabby friar who stands near the road, watching the procession with the concentration of a lion studying a herd of antelope; nor does he hear the grumbles and low curses of the soldiers when the fellow makes his decision and dives into the ranks as into a river, fighting the current with powerful strokes of his arms and dodging the hooves of the horses by a sprightly dance that brings him closer and closer to the emperor's side.

So the emperor is taken entirely by surprise when a strong hand suddenly grasps his stirrup and another grips his ankle. He lets out a soft cry of dismay as he looks down into the face of a wild man. His beard and hair are laced with sticks and leaves, his dark eyes are mad with purpose: his mouth moves frantically, he is making some prophecy. Even as two guards seize the man by his shoulders and drag him away, the emperor bends to hear what he is saying, and he does hear it; the words assail him as if they are being shouted inside his head. "Repent while you still live, for your glory cannot last. False riches will not make you heir to the kingdom of God. The mighty of this earth shall be as beggars before God's judgment, your days of glory are numbered, they will not last. We serve Lady Poverty . . ."

The procession goes on. The emperor does not look back to see the wild man, who lies on his back in the ditch where the soldiers have thrown him, muttering cheerfully into the empty air, "Your glory will not last."

An Importunate Novice

*You cannot tell what degree of patience and humility
a servant of God has about him as long as he has
been having his way.*

—ST. FRANCIS OF ASSISI
"The Admonitions"

Illuminato is ill, he can scarcely hold down a sprig of parsley, and Francesco is not much better; his old fever has returned, and he alternates between burning, sweating, and shivering. For two nights they sleep in the fields, waking up hungry and parched to the bright chatter of the birds. Unlike these carefree creatures, flitting about on their daily business, the friars are barely able to stand. They beg alms in every town along the way and work for two days, one for a farmer bringing in hay and another for a baker in Spoleto, stacking wood. They see many sights and are accosted by all manner of people. A French knight speaks to them of his travels; a trio of brigands, finding they have nothing to steal, beats them severely, leaving Illuminato with a swollen wrist and a bruised face. One night they stay in a *laʒaretto*, and Francesco shares a straw mat with a putrid, stinking fellow whose hospitality he repays in the morning with a cool bath. Illuminato, who has slept out under the stars, carries the water up from the stream and leans in the doorway of the hovel to watch this operation. The noisy children of the place crowd in around his legs. He joins Francesco in a song, to the delight of the company, but he cannot bring himself to go inside, and for this failing he reproaches himself bitterly.

At Terni they hear an excellent troubadour and see a slave dead in the stocks. The townspeople tell them the man has stolen his master's shirt and worn it to the market, as if he thought no one would notice. At Marmore they sleep near the falls and dream all night to the sound of rushing water. A boar chases them across a vineyard, and when the farmer sees them waving their arms and shouting, he comes out and kills the beast with only his eating knife. Then, pleased with the friars for bringing the boar, which has been despoiling his crops and tearing up his grapevines for weeks, he offers them a place to sleep in his shed and sends a boy with bread, cheese, meat, and the recommendation that they eat as many grapes as they want before going on. It is Francesco's opinion the grapes will cure Illuminato, and in truth he does not vomit them up, but they turn his bowels to water, and he spends the night squatting in the dirt outside the shed.

It rains all one day and is cloudy the next, so their robes do not dry out. When Francesco begins to preach to two laborers fighting on the road, they leave off pummeling each other and turn on him, beating him about the head while he shouts God's praises and Illuminato stands by weeping and imploring them, for the love of God, to spare this holy man, Brother Francesco, the father of all the Fratres Minores. But it is fatigue and not the love of God that finally persuades them to stop. Without an apology, or even a word of farewell, they leave the two friars and go off together talking amiably, their quarrel evidently forgotten.

In this way, at last, Francesco and Illuminato arrive at Greccio, and all the friars come running out to welcome them. The *custos*, finding them damp, bruised, and ill, escorts them to the dining room, where a pot of soup bubbles upon the fire. Gratefully, they accept the loan of dry tunics from this *custos*, a short, chubby, mirthful fellow who exchanges witticisms with Illuminato on the pleasures of travel. Francesco sinks down near the fire and bids Illuminato to do the same and to have at once a bowl of the soup which will surely mend his stomach. Then the *custos* announces that a novice has arrived that morning, seeking Francesco, because he has some special permission to ask of him.

How many times is he to be accosted by this vain and ridiculous young man? When they left Borgo San Sepolcro this fellow followed them out to the road. No sooner have they arrived at Greccio than he has turned up again, determined to renew his urgent petition to the holy father.

The novice has demonstrated, the *custos* admits, that he can read the Psalter, albeit haltingly, with curious lapses in pronunciation and the toneless accent of a schoolboy, but he thinks he reads excellently and has somehow extracted from his minister permission to have a psalter of his own. Then, of course, some of his fellow friars have told him that Father Francesco expressly forbids the friars to own books, so he has gotten it into his head that he will have no peace with his until Francesco gives him a special dispensation to have it.

Francesco sits with his head in his hands, listening patiently. Illuminato mutters over his soup bowl, "This fellow should go and join the Benedictines."

"Send him in," Francesco says.

The *custos* goes out, returning almost at once with the agitated novice, a handsome young man with a self-important air, though before this august audience he adopts a humble manner so absurdly transparent it makes Illuminato and the *custos* exchange looks of thinly veiled merriment. Francesco studies the boy with interest, as if he has never met such a promising example of Christian virtue. He says nothing, nor could he if he wished to, for the novice immediately launches into the argument he has been working over in his brain all the way from San Sepolcro, explaining why, in his particular case, because of his great love of the word of God and his ability to read it, and his great pleasure in reading it, and the virtue that accrues to his soul by that reading and to the souls of those who, when the occasion allows, might hear his reading and be improved by it, so that even his own minister has agreed that he must profit by it, it can do no harm to his soul nor show forth an example of wickedness or vanity, but rather must show his true simplicity and love of the Divine Word, if he were allowed to have, for the improvement of his own devotion and that of his brothers in Christ, a psalter of his own.

Francesco does not cease his close attention to the novice, who seems to bask and preen beneath the father's eye, like a peacock before a bevy of attentive hens. Illuminato concentrates on his soup; the *custos* has taken a seat on a low stool near the fire, his back to the interview so that his amusement may not be seen. At last the novice reaches his peroration and stands quietly stroking his beard, his eyes lowered, ready to accept the opinion of the wise and loving father.

"You know it is against our rule," Francesco says, "for any friar to possess more than one tunic, quilted if he likes, a cord, and breeches?"

The eager eyes dart upward, engaging momentarily a directness of inquiry that makes it impossible for him to say more than "Yes, Father."

Francesco leans away from the youth and holds his hands out to the fire as if he might solicit a decision from it. He turns his hands palm-down, warming them, and speaks in a voice heavy with fatigue. "If you have a psalter," he says, "then you will want a breviary. And when you have a breviary, you will sit in your stall like a grand prelate and say to your brother, 'Hand me my breviary.'"

Francesco rises to his feet. The novice steps back and manages a feeble protest which dies in his throat. Francesco kneels at the hearth, his back to the youth, takes up a handful of ashes and, raising his hand high, pours the ashes over his own head. Illuminato looks on curiously, and the *custos*, alerted by the sudden, ponderous silence behind him, turns on his stool to watch. Francesco rubs the ashes down over his forehead, then around his cheeks and over his chin as if washing himself. "I, a breviary," he says, closing his eyes, intoning, like a chant. "I, a breviary." And he repeats this action and this phrase until the novice, alarmed and thoroughly perplexed, slowly backs away and lets himself out of the door he came in.

A Friar Damned

When the craving for moral consistency and purity is developed to this degree, the subject may well find the outer world too full of shocks to dwell in, and can unify his life and keep his soul unspotted only by withdrawing from it. That law which impels the artist to achieve harmony in his composition by simply dropping out whatever jars, or suggests a discord, rules also in the spiritual life. . . . So monasteries and communities of sympathetic devotees open their doors, and in their changeless order, characterized by omissions quite as much as constituted of actions, the holy-minded person finds that inner smoothness and cleanness which it is torture to him to feel violated at every turn by the discordancy and brutality of secular existence.

—WILLIAM JAMES
The Varieties of Religious Experience

It has rained for five days and nights. In the valley the sun breaks through the clouds now and then, but at the mountain hermitage where the friars have removed for a period of prayer and meditation, the clouds never part. When the rain lightens, a gray mist rises from the sodden ground to the low gray ceiling overhead. Gray friars in gray weather. Francesco is troubled by prognosticating dreams. Every time he closes his eyes, he looks into a world of treachery and despair, not just for himself but for all the friars. He wakes up shouting. Leone has heard him from his cell which is nearby.

Brother Elia has not noticed what the others cannot help seeing: Francesco is avoiding him. If Francesco is walking on the forest path and Elia approaches, he takes the first turning. At supper he chooses a place facing away from Elia, and when the friars recite the hours, he is careful to choose the rank behind Elia. Elia, as usual, is absorbed in his schemes and in his reading, for against Francesco's express decree, he has had several books delivered to him, borrowed from the bishop's library. Gradually, as the rain beats down and forces them all into one another's company, as tempers fray and the cook struggles over yet another pot of the poorest pottage, even Elia becomes aware of the reticence of his friend. It comes to him all at once one morning when he wakes from a sound and dreamless sleep—Francesco will not look at him.

Elia is a man who never acts impulsively. Before he speaks, he tests his theory. First he approaches Francesco in the yard near the refectory, where he is walking up and down in the rain, but as soon as Elia is near enough to speak, Francesco turns away and goes out quickly by the wooden gate, in the direction of his cell. Later, when Elia is leaving the chapel, he sees Francesco on the path coming toward him, his head bowed under the weight of his damp cowl, and he calls out to him, "Brother, God give you peace." Francesco whirls in his tracks as if suddenly remembering some important matter and disappears around the corner of the building. Elia follows, darting into the rain, then stops, too baffled and hurt for pursuit. What could he have done to deserve such treatment?

At vespers he observes how Francesco avoids him, and at dinner, when they all sit down to the unappetizing mess in their bowls—the only good thing about it is that there is not much of it—Elia takes a place across from Francesco and tries to engage his attention by staring at him. Though Elia's neighbors cast one another curious looks, Francesco keeps his eyes on his bowl, eating steadily and mopping up the last bits with a hard crust of bread. Elia tries to eat as well, but the stuff is so vile it nauseates him and he offers his half-full bowl to his neighbor Angelo, who accepts with his habitual grace. As Elia scrapes the mess into his brother's bowl, Angelo bends upon him a look of sympathy that galls him. Is he the subject of the friars' tiresome gossip? Is he the only one who does not know why Francesco is not speaking to Elia? Francesco leans against Leone's shoulder and whispers into his ear. Leone smiles and nods. Anger seizes Elia hard and fast as a wolf's jaws. He grinds his teeth, pushing away the empty bowl, and reaches out across the table to catch Francesco's sleeve, but he misses, for Francesco is rising from his seat. His eyes rest momentarily on the outstretched hand, then he turns away.

"Father." Elia hears his own voice, too loud and querulous, but he cannot modulate it. "How have I offended you?"

Francesco appears not to hear this question, though the rest of the assembly stop speaking and give Elia their undivided attention, which inflames his determination to receive an answer, here, before them all, so that there will be no more rumors, nothing one brother saw and another heard patched together in a shabby filthy quilt like the one Francesco is pulling at as he walks resolutely toward the door. Elia resists the urge to leap over the table. Instead, he makes his way around it, gripping the edge at one corner and banging his hip cruelly on the other. "Father," he says, catching up to Francesco just as he raises his hand to the door latch. "Tell me in what manner I have offended you."

The hand neither hastens nor relents from the operation of lifting the latch. In the next moment, Francesco will pass through the doorway.

Something hot and red floods into the brain of Brother Elia, so sudden and dislocating that he clutches the bridge of his nose with one hand while with the other he catches Francesco's arm just above the elbow and bears down hard. "Francesco," he says. "Answer me. Why do you avoid me? Why won't you look at me?"

Francesco cannot leave, but he does not turn from the door. Not even time moves in the room—the two men at the doorway, behind them the long table where the friars on their benches, some seated, some half-standing, are frozen in various gestures, one with a bit of bread raised halfway to his lips, another bending down to scratch his ankle. The bitter reproach of the questions echoes in the air. Slowly Francesco releases the latch, slowly he turns, his arm still entrapped by his interlocutor, who does not relinquish his hold. "Because, Elia," Francesco says, his voice firm and loud enough for the entire breathless audience to hear, "it has been revealed to me that you are damned."

Elia, dumbfounded, releases Francesco and takes a step backward as if he has received a blow, and indeed he has. He is dear to Francesco, he is certain of this. He has served him and loved him almost from the start. Astonished, bitter tears rise to his eyes, his heart races, a terrible incapacitating panic sweeps him to his knees. "For the love of Christ," he cries out. "Don't drive me away, Francesco!"

Behind him, the friars have turned into a wall of eyes and ears, entirely focused upon the scene: Elia, the proud, the worldly, the learned intellectual, weeping over the bare feet of Francesco, a man who cannot write five words of Latin without mistaking two. Francesco does not move away as he might, but looks down on the humbled, shaken man at his feet, who is begging for his mercy, for his intercession. "If I were lying in the deepest pit of hell," Elia implores, "and you prayed for me, I know I would be relieved." He raises his head, dashing the tears from his eyes with rough strokes, then presses his forehead against the cold floor. "Francesco, I beg you to pray for me, recommend me, a sinner, don't turn away from me, I beg you."

Francesco says nothing. A fresh flood of tears overwhelms Elia, his bowed shoulders tremble with helpless sobs; he chokes and gasps for breath. Francesco looks down upon him, but distantly, with a mild perplexity of expression, as if he is engaged in some puzzling botanical question, a plant he cannot, exactly, identify, a berry that might or might not be poisonous. Reluctantly, tentatively, he bends over the weeping man and rests his hand on the crown of his head. "Very well," he says, "I will pray for you."

On His Simplicity

Brother Fire Desires a Blanket

If we owned anything, we should have to have weapons to protect ourselves. That is what gives rise to contentions and lawsuits, and so often causes the love of God and neighbor to be interfered with. For ourselves, we are resolved to possess nothing temporal in this world.

——ST. FRANCIS OF ASSISI
Legend of the Three Companions

When the weather turned cold, the count sent sheepskins; now, because it is not a meatless day, his hunters have come up from the valley with a bag of pheasants for the friars' dinner. Lying beneath a skin by the fire in the mud-patched hut, Francesco is thoughtful. They are too comfortable, he warns, but it would not be courteous to refuse the count's generosity, since it is by his care and affection for the friars that he is piling up treasure for his own soul in heaven. Leone sits on the floor plucking the birds. The smoke drifts over their heads and out the door. This mountain is a sacred place, Francesco continues. It has been revealed to him as he prayed that the mountain was thrust up on the plain at the same moment the rocks on Mount Calvary were riven and the Lord Christ descended into hell to free those souls who had not known him. At the mention of the unholy regions, the fire flares up, and sparks fly onto the dirt floor. Francesco is too close, so Leone motions him back, then, realizing his gesture is lost upon his nearly sightless friend, he says, "Francesco, be careful."

The fire flares again; a spark flies into the dry thatch of the ceiling. "Lord have mercy on us," Leone exclaims. At once a thin line of flame appears, leaping across the central beam with a whoosh of hot breath at the apex, then winding down the floor beam in a gyre, like a flight of red and golden birds. Leone leaps up as quickly as the fire, pulls off his tunic, and flails it frantically against the post. "Help me," he cries, glancing over his shoulder to see Francesco, who is standing just outside the door, suddenly dart back inside, take up his sheepskin, and run out again. "Angelo," Leone shouts, "Rufino, come at once. Our little house is burning."

He has no hope of being heard; his brothers' hut is out of earshot, but calling their names comforts him as he dances about the hut in his breeches, whirling his tunic this way and that while the smoke rises, choking and blinding him. He struggles on, and then he hears a welcome sound: the shouts of his brothers, and in a few moments Angelo and Rufino burst into the room wielding their clothes. The three wage a brief battle in which they all commend themselves to Christ's mercy, then they beat the insurgent flames into submission and confine the cooking fire to its rightful circle of stones. The friars stand laughing, sweating, and praising God for sparing the pheasants, as they now all have a great appetite. Leone asks if Francesco warned them of his peril. He did not, Rufino replies. "Brother Angelo spied the smoke through the trees when he went down to the stream to wash his feet. He shouted to me and we came running, but we didn't see Francesco."

"He ran out," Leone says, looking at the doorway, "when the fire started."

They take their places on the ground, and Leone recommences plucking the birds. They talk of Francesco's reverence for Brother Fire, of his refusal even to snuff a candle. Rufino recalls a night in the early days at Rivo Torto, when he woke up in the dark and cried out, "I am dying." "Francesco got up and lit the lamp," he says, "and asked us, 'Which is the one who said, I am dying?'"

Leone stops pulling at the bird and listens. Rivo Torto was before his time, and he likes to hear the stories of the early brotherhood, when Francesco was young and finding his own way. "I confessed that I had spoken," Rufino continues, "that I was dying of hunger. I had eaten only one piece of bread in two days."

Angelo smiles, recalling those times. "No one was sending pheasants at Rivo Torto," he observes.

Rufino nods in agreement. "So, Francesco woke everyone and made us all get up. He took the poor stores we had, set them out on the board, and shared them out to each, so that I might not be embarrassed to eat alone. And when we had eaten, he told us that we should each consider our own nature and that some among us might need more food than others, but that we should shun too much abstinence as we would shun gluttony."

"If only he would take his own advice," Leone observes.

Rufino agrees, then reverts to his story. "When we were finished, we got back into our places, each under our own name. I moved to put out the light, and Francesco said no, he couldn't bear to hurt Brother Fire. So the lamp burned all night until the oil had run out, and it was a week before we had a light again."

Angelo has another story, one Rufino has not heard, but Leone, who was there, remembers it well. As soon as Angelo says it was at the hermitage in Fonte Colombo, Leone chuckles. "We were sitting around the fire," Angelo begins, "just as we are now, and a spark flew into Francesco's robe. In a moment the fire began to climb up the hem of his tunic. I was sitting next to him, and when I saw it, I shouted, 'Francesco, your tunic is burning!' and I tried to put out the fire with my hands. But he backed away, and he said, 'Oh, do not harm Brother Fire.'"

"He's flaming up like a torch," Leone puts in.

"What could we do?" Angelo continues. "Stand by and watch him burn alive? He made absolutely no effort to save himself. Finally we were obliged to break our vow of obedience and beat Brother Fire with feed sacks. Francesco was desolate."

Their talk goes on. The sun is setting, the birds are cleaned and speared on skewers Rufino has cut from a sapling. They hear footsteps rustling the leaves outside. Francesco appears in the smoky doorway, clutching his sheepskin and frowning. The friars call out, "Father, Father, come and sit by the fire." He enters, holding the skin out before him, his expression contrite, as if it is all he can do to keep from falling on his knees and begging God's mercy for his grievous fault. He goes to Angelo and drops the sheepskin into his lap. "I do not want to have this skin over me anymore," he explains, "since through my avarice I did not want Brother Fire to eat it." And then he turns, shrugs, and smiles. He squats on the ground near Leone, who is shaking his head in amusement, and, stretching his arms over his knees, holds his hands out to the warmth of the fire.

Demons in a Tower

Demons unsettle the senses, stir low passions, disorder life, cause alarms in sleep, bring diseases, fill the mind with terror, distort the limbs, control the way lots are cast, make a pretence at oracles by their tricks, arouse the passion of love, create the heat of cupidity, lurk in consecrated images.

—ISIDORE OF SEVILLE
Differentiae

Bernardo shields his eyes with his palm as he gazes at the tower jutting above the ramparts of the city wall. The white stones dazzle his weary eyes; he did not sleep even one hour the night before. With his back to the tower, Francesco looks out over the city, arms folded across his chest to protect him from the cold wind that has been blowing incessantly now for several days. It was because of the wind that Cardinal Leo offered this tower, promising the friars they could stay here, just as in a hermitage. His custom was to lodge any number of poor men and women, and the friars would not be guests or retainers, but only two among the many who accepted the cardinal's charity, thereby recommending him to God and man.

And so Francesco inspected the tower and found it private and retired, with nine vaulted rooms furnished simply with beds, plain benches and tables, wide polished steps, many windows giving fine vistas of the Tevere and the ancient tomb of the emperor Hadrian, and even water from a cistern on the roof piped in to every floor. He pronounced it a most pleasing spot and agreed to spend some days in meditation and prayer, until the wind should abate and the friars might walk back to Fonte Colombo.

If he had known what waited for him in the tower, Francesco gladly would have braved the gale, coupled with God's icy rain or snow, as he has many times before, contented, joyful to be wandering, as the Lord Christ did, abandoned by men and relying on God's mercy to bring him to shelter. When he consented to stay in Cardinal Leo's tower, unbeknownst to him, he turned away from that divine mercy and cut himself off from salvation, for no sooner had night fallen in that place than a tiny demon appeared on the window ledge, the scout of his band. Francesco, who stood beside the bed reciting his prayers, thought at first it was some oversized horsefly. He went at once to observe this marvel, but when he was closer he saw the sharp, leathery wings, the stubby horns, and the goatish feet which the creature stamped about. It spewed forth foul curses and made a lewd display of its naked, hairy buttocks.

Francesco backed away, calling on God's mercy, and the creature made a barking sound as if in imitation, calling on his own master, who was the prince of hell. Then another creature appeared beside him, as big as a bird and much like a bat except for its strong furred legs with sharp black hooves and its sharp black teeth that jutted past its jaws, like bars on a cage. Francesco felt a terror such as he had never known, not in the tumult of battle, when he was still his father's son and wore the colors of his Commune to the field, nor in the dark prison of Perugia, where he saw a prisoner forced to take toads into his mouth until he choked and died, nor when he renounced the world and fell into the hands of thieves who beat him and left him for dead in a snowy ditch. The second demon summoned a third, as big as a hawk; the third called upon a fourth, the size of a young pig, its face covered in matted hair and with red eyes like two hot coals; and so on, until they spilled over the sill into the room, howling and cursing God. Francesco closed his eyes—surely this was a dream—but when he opened them again, the demons were gathered around him, snorting and shoving one another like maddened beasts. One of them caught the hem of Francesco's robe and yanked him to his knees. Then the others all fell upon him, kicking and biting, shouting curses, beating him about the face, pressing their stinking flesh against his mouth and nose, until he wept and cried out, "Bernardo, come at once. Come and save me."

A demon like a monkey with short horns that looked raw and soft leaped up before Francesco, slapping his face so hard he lost his footing and fell against the wall. He shouted, "Help, help,

Bernardo!" A demon with dugs like an old sow's and a swollen red pubis leaped over his chest and, holding him by the beard, banged his head once, twice, against the stone floor. Through the roar of the demons, he heard the sound of the door scraping the floor, then Bernardo's head appeared, peering into the darkness, confused by sleep. In the same moment the demons disappeared.

Francesco lay on his back, his limbs trembling, his hands still battling his attackers. "Brother," he cried, "come and stay by me, for I am afraid to be alone in this place."

Bernardo went at once to his side and helped him to sit up. "What happened to you?" he asked. Francesco whispered, "Demons." He clung to Bernardo's arm, his teeth chattering, his breath harsh and rapid. When the moon broke from a cloud and poured its light through the casement, Bernardo saw that his friend's face was bruised, and there were scratches, such as a cat might leave in trying to escape a captor, all along his neck and on his mouth. "Do not leave me," he repeated.

"I won't," Bernardo promised. They sat in silence, listening for any sound. Francesco shuddered each time he glanced toward the window where the demons had appeared.

"Why did the demons beat me?" he asked in a voice so aggrieved and piteous that Bernardo patted his shoulder. "I don't know, Francesco," he said gently.

The hours passed one by one while the two friars sat together in the dark chamber, waiting for the first light of day. When a night bird alighted in the window, Francesco clutched Bernardo, burying his face in his shoulder, but when the bird gave its familiar plaintive note, he lifted his head and murmured a prayer of thanksgiving. They calculated that it was past the midnight hour, so they recited their morning prayers, hoping to hasten the dawn. Soon Francesco's fear gave way to thoughtfulness. Why had the demons come? Why had God, in his grace and mercy, given them power to harm his faithful servant? "Demons are God's constables," Francesco said at last. "Just as the podesta, when someone offends, sends his constable to punish him, so God chastises and corrects those he loves through his police. Many times, even a perfect religious can sin through ignorance."

"This is certainly true," Bernardo agreed.

"It may be, it seems to me, that God punishes me through his police because, although the cardinal willingly does me this kindness, and my body needs to accept and I feel I may confidently accept it from him, my brothers who go through the world bearing hunger and many tribulations, and other brothers who live in wretched houses and hermitages, when they hear that I stay with a cardinal, may have occasion to murmur against me, saying 'We suffer so many privations and he has his comforts.' " Francesco nodded his head slowly, approving his own skillful reasoning. "So I am bound always to give them a good example, as I was given to them especially for this."

"But what can you do now," Bernardo asked, "since you have accepted the cardinal's invitation?"

"I will go to him as soon as it is light, and I will tell him what I have told you. And I will say to him, 'Men have great faith in me and believe me to be a holy man, and lo, demons have thrown me out of my cell.' " He laughed and stretched out his legs, yawning.

And that is exactly what he will say, Bernardo thinks now as he gazes up at the tower. The cardinal will accept this excuse, and Bernardo and Francesco will be back on the road to Fonte Colombo that very day. After their long journey, the friars there will receive them warmly, they will tell this story of the demons who beat Father Francesco without mercy, and all will express satisfaction at his miraculous escape.

Bernardo turns to look at Francesco, who is pointing to the sky. The demons seem far from his thoughts; he has spotted an eagle gliding slowly on a current of air, the powerful wings outstretched, the feathers at the tips quivering slightly, the head and talons dropped beneath the body, the golden eyes scouring the earth far below.

Bernardo joins Francesco. An eagle is a rare sight in Roma these days, though he has heard that in the time of the Lord Christ they were not uncommon. The two friars watch the bird wheeling in a slow circle above their heads. Then the great bird breaks his circle and soars off toward the city. The friars make their way across the ramparts to the steps that lead down inside the wall. At the entry, Bernardo looks back one last time at the tower. What is it that he sees hanging over the ledge of the window near the top? Is it a bit of rope? Or perhaps someone has forgotten a black robe hung out to dry in the sun. He blinks to clear his vision, then looks again. It is black, it is moving, but it doesn't seem to be at the mercy of the wind; rather, it moves against it. As he watches, it splits into two pieces and he can make it out clearly, a wing like a bat's but too big, and the other part a black arm ending in something like a foot. He covers his eyes and turns away to follow Father Francesco down into the dark stairway.

A Snow Family

If the Devil can get hold of a single hair of a person, he soon has it enlarged to a cable. And if for years on end he is not able to down the person he has been tempting, he does not haggle over the delay so long as the person gives in to him in the end. That is his business. He thinks of nothing else day and night.

—ST. FRANCIS OF ASSISI
The Second Life of St. Francis

The snow started in the morning as the friars were singing in their chapel. They came out to find the network of paths leading to their huts dusted with white. The sky was white, and the snowflakes drifted down through the dark branches of the trees, gathering in the crooks of the limbs and in the thicker tufts of the pines. The night before had been bitterly cold, but it was warmer now, and the beauty of the falling snow, the hush of it, made the friars smile at one another. They joked, as they parted, about who had the flimsiest roof and who would wake up to find himself beneath a blanket of snow.

All day the snow continued, falling thickly and steadily, until the footpaths disappeared and the huts and chapel were piled high. A farmer had given Brother Pacifico some beans, and Brother Rufino was trying to cook them with onions and a cabbage he had grown himself, but the snow was falling into his pot and he couldn't keep the fire hot enough to hold a boil. The wind picked up, lifting the snow and swirling it about in flimsy tornados that skittered among the bushes and across the clearing where the friars took their meals. Then, just as the beans began to boil and the two friars who had gone begging in the town came struggling out of the forest, their robes tucked up into their breeches, singing the praises of Lady Poverty and calling out the bounty they carried in their sack—bread, three eggs, one entire fish—the snow stopped.

At vespers the air was icy and sharp in the friars' nostrils, and the steam of their breath rose heavenward with their voices. When they gathered for the meal, the sky was as clear and cold as a sheet of black ice, and the air was still. Brother Pacifico took a broom and swept the stones near the fire, and Francesco, taking up two sticks, danced behind him, wielding his sticks like a *vielle* and singing a French song about the trials of love. His high spirits, combined with the warmth of the blaze, the tempting aromas of the soup and the fish roasting in the coals under the pot, infected them with good humor. Praise and blessings were heaped upon the head of the fisherman who had spoken kindly to the two friars. He had told them he caught so many fish that day, he had made up his mind to save one for the Poor Men, and here they were, on the road as he returned to his home, just as if the Lord had sent them.

After they had eaten every morsel of fish, scraped the soup pot of every last bean, and consumed every crumb of bread, no matter how stale or crusty, Francesco spoke to them of Christ the fisherman casting out his nets to catch souls for heaven, and how they did the same by their example, so that this fisherman, having received that day the proof of God's infinite love and providence for his children, reserved a portion for those he knew to be, as the Lord Christ himself had chosen to be, humble and poor. The friars listened dreamily. Francesco's voice wrapped all around them in the chilly night air, and when he had finished, for several moments a devout silence held them still there, in the clearing, with the fire burning low, and all around the forest, black and white, stretching up to the black starry night bending over them all.

Now it is after midnight. The friars are asleep in their huts, feet tucked into their robes, hands hidden in their sleeves, cowls pulled closed about their sleeping faces. But Brother Illuminato cannot sleep. He leans in the doorway of his shelter, looking out at the opposite hillside. The moon is full and sheds its light upon the white landscape which reflects it, so that the air itself seems bright, suffused with a pale light, not warm, like daylight, but charged and magical, like the cool, all-seeing light that might pour from the eyes of God.

When he looks to his right, Illuminato can see Francesco's hut. Is he asleep? Or is he, like this brother, too restless for sleep, drawn to his door by the nacreous glow of the moon and too enchanted by the scene outside to lie down again on his mat? Brother Angelo has told him that Francesco never sleeps; he prays all night. And sometimes he is tortured by devils, so that he appears in the morning exhausted and bruised from his struggles. Illuminato peers toward Francesco's doorway, and as he does, suddenly, the door flies open and Francesco himself bursts out as if shot from a catapult. Illuminato rubs his eyes; does he see what he thinks he sees? There is the blessed father, without a shred of clothes, his hair wild about his face, his arms flailing over his head as if he is plagued by insects, his feet beating down the snow in a mad dance. Illuminato can see dark red stripes on the pale skin of his back. Francesco throws himself upon the snow, first on his bleeding back, groaning deep, sensual, animal groans, like a dog luxuriating in carrion. Then he rolls over on his stomach, raises his upper body on outstretched arms, his head dropped forward between his shoulders, and drags himself, bare legs limp behind him, in a long circle, out to the snow-laden currant bush and back again to his starting place.

Illuminato cannot contain his curiosity. Indeed, he is moved in part by fear, for surely Francesco is in the hands of invisible devils, just as Angelo said he was, and if they torture the father to such a frenzy as this, what might they do to a poor unworthy friar who comes between them and their prey? Stealthily, he crosses the yard, and when he has reached the cover of the currant bush, he drops to his hands and knees to peek.

Francesco is seated, his bloody back turned to Illuminato. He is gathering the snow all around him, occupied, like a boy building a snow fortress, in rolling it into a ball. He gets up on his knees and pulls in more snow, making more balls, bigger and bigger ones, and setting them all around him. He arranges them carefully, tamping down the snow at the base, until, apparently satisfied, he sits back, his legs splayed out before him, surrounded by a semi-circle of snow heaps. Illuminato sinks down beneath his bush, barely breathing, for Francesco is speaking and he can make out the words, though their sense escapes him. Francesco addresses the snow heaps solemnly: "This big one is your wife," he says, "and these four your two sons and your two daughters; the other two are your servant and your maid, whom you must have to serve you." He puts a subtle, ironic emphasis on the word "must." Then he is silent, considering his new family. He smiles, and a sound starts deep in his chest, a laugh being suppressed, and Illuminato is smiling too, for it is so very odd of him, the holy father, the inspiration and guide of so many brothers, to sit naked in the snow in the middle of the night, addressing himself to snowballs.

The laugh pushes harder and Francesco cannot control it, it bursts out hearty and loud like a donkey braying. He scrambles to his feet. "Hurry," he says, "hurry and clothe them all, for they are dying of the cold." This observation brings a renewed gale of laughter; he is bent in half by the force of it. He drops to his knees, stumbles back to his feet, laughing helplessly, and Illuminato has to put his hands over his own mouth, for this laughter, so free of self-consciousness and full of delight, is contagious. Francesco rises to his feet, looks about him at his snow family, still chuckling but calmer now. Before he walks away, he stretches out his arms to the gorgeous, gleaming moon pouring down whiteness over him like milk. "*Jubilate Deo,*" he sings, softly, with a tender lingering over the melodic twisting of the plainsong: Ju-oo-bee-ee-lah-ah-tay-eh-day-eh-o. Illuminato rests his chin on his palms and mouths the words, his eyes mesmerized by the naked back of Francesco, who walks solemnly past his snow family without looking back, goes singing into his hut, and kicks the door closed behind him.

On His Travels to the Holy Land

At the Harbor

God! We have for so long been brave in idleness! Now we shall see who will be truly brave; and we shall go to avenge the doleful shame at which every man ought to be downcast and sorrowful, for in our times the holy places have been lost, where God suffered death in anguish for us; if we now permit our mortal enemies to stay there, our lives will be shameful for evermore.

—CONON OF BÉTHUNE
"Ahi, Amours! come dure departie"

The gray friars crowd together on the dock, gawking at the ships moored in the harbor, more ships than there are friars in the world, bobbing on their lines, great and small, plain barks and galleys with a hundred oar, catos weighed down by siege engines and lumber, long ships with crenelated castles at each end like floating cities, ships with blood-red sails trimmed in gold above and below the water line, ships awaiting cargo and ships being loaded, their decks littered with helmets, shields, cooking pots, bags of biscuit, dried fish, spears and battle-axes, ships like glittering stars in the blue expanse of roiling sea, which is as deep as the sky is high and ends in the Holy Land.

Francesco stands apart from the group, speaking to a party of knights whose red crosses and haughty bearing proclaim that they have heard God's call to arms in France and come down over land to take ship at Ancona. Francesco is eager to practice his French, for they say the sultan keeps a Frenchman ever at his side to translate his messages to the Franj. The knights are big men; they tower over the poor friar, but they bend their necks to hear him, for they know he is the leader of the Minores, famous throughout Christendom for his virtue and beloved of the Lord Pope Innocent of holy memory, and of Innocent's successor, old Honorius, who has taken up the keys to Christ's kingdom and directs the holy war against the infidel. The knights nod and pull their beards; Brother Francesco's French is courtly, but not always correct. A shout goes up from the friars, whose lives are endangered by a pair of rearing, stamping horses, terrified of the sea and determined to break away from their handler, a wiry, dark youth who wears a scarf over his head like a Saracen, though he shouts at the horses in guttural

French. Francesco takes his leave of the knights and returns to his anxious flock.

When he left the Portiuncula, he had only Illuminato as his companion, but on their travels they have been joined by a lively band of friars who want nothing more than to accompany their blessed father to martyrdom in the holy lands, or if Christ's army is triumphant, then they might live to see the Holy Sepulchre freed from the Saracens. The French knights have spoken to Francesco of the true cross, which has fallen into the hands of the sultan, as well as other precious relics, the bones, hearts, and tongues of the saints, so defiled they call out for rescue, and the Lord Pope has heard their cry. King Jean is even now at Damietta, that fortress city which is the doorway to the Nile, where the brave knights of diverse kingdoms have laid siege for a year and the sultan al-Kamil, with his warrior-slaves and his retinue of servants and sorcerers, is camped behind the city. Here the liberation of Jerusalem must begin, and it will surely take place as soon as the emperor Frederick, the Hammer of the World, who has taken the cross in the presence of the Lord Pope, fulfills his promise and arrives with his forces on the Egyptian shore.

The sun beats down on the crowded dock, and the hot wind stings the friars' eyes. Illuminato, who has gone to search among the ships for one that will take their company, makes his way through a band of ragged children; they shout at him and call him "pissintunic" and other foul names, but he smiles upon them, patting their dirty necks as he pushes through. When he reaches the friars, he says, "There is one who will take us, but he has room only for twelve and he sails within the hour." At this news, they are all downcast, and each one shows on his face the wish that he might not be left behind. "I cannot choose among you," Francesco says. He calls out to the children, "One of you, come to our aid and God will bless you." Two surly, curious boys separate from their peers and strut about the friars, their arms entwined, whispering to each other. The taller boy addresses himself to

Francesco—what will the friars give them for this service? Francesco laughs. The friars have nothing to give, he explains, they are beggars, just as the boy is, and as the Lord Christ was on this earth; but if he agrees to help them, he will feel the breath of God moving through him, and that is a greater reward than riches. The boy shrugs, as if he felt already the divine exhalation. "What is the task?" he says.

"From these friars, you must choose eleven who will go with me to the Holy Land to preach among the infidel."

The friars crowd closely around the boy, who has lost all his surliness and looks from one to the other as gravely as a judge upon his high seat. "I choose this one," he says, going to a young friar near the back and touching his sleeve. The brothers step away from the chosen one, and one murmurs that this selection is truly inspired by God, for this brother, Ugo, is renowned for his humility and devotion to the Holy Cross. The boy ponders the group, then takes the hand of the friar nearest him, who is Illuminato. "And this one," the boy says.

"Illuminato," Francesco sighs. "I knew you would be with me on this journey."

Then another friar is chosen, and another, and at each one the friars confess they feel the righteousness of God's own hand in the matter. The boy hardly glances at his companion, who stands nearby, nodding as each friar is called forth. The last is Brother Pietro, a pious, educated friar from Le Marche who was once a powerful knight and a *crucesignato*, having taken the cross in Roma. On hearing Father Francesco speak in the market of his town, this nobleman turned over all his wealth, his houses, and his lands to repay his debt to the Lord Pope, and took on the habit of the friars. So Christ called him first to arms and now to prayer and poverty in the dangerous kingdom of the infidel.

Francesco entreats those who must stay behind to pray for those who go, that they may be, like the knights, true defenders of the cross. He blesses them each, then bids Illuminato to lead the way to their ship.

They proceed in single file, as is their custom, winding among the clutches of knights, the tradesmen pushing their barrows piled high with bags of grain and cabbages, the hills of rope and communities of barrels, ever closer to the sea. Illuminato points to the ship's black hull, which looms above a steep gangplank on which a steady stream of sweating humanity—porters laden down with chests, sailors pulling along pigs or struggling with braces of squawking chickens, women carrying stacks of blankets and linens, boys nearly hidden by shields, wineskins, enormous loaves of black bread—clambers steadily upward. The friars line up, laughing nervously, and Illuminato directs Francesco's gaze to the wooden tower midships where the captain looks serenely upon the noise and confusion below, his long golden beard fluttering like an oriflamme. Illuminato waves and waves until he catches the captain's attention, then points at Francesco, whose passage the captain has agreed to because he knows God will not harm this famous holy man; and so the ship, which seems to the friars like a floating palace but is in his mind as flimsy and imperiled as a sinner's soul before the final judgment, will arrive safely at the port of Acre. The captain gives a call to the sailor perched in the crow's nest above him. The sailor takes up a horn and blows a single thrilling note. Far below the decks, an oarsman lifts his head to hear the sound, then, rubbing his callused hands together, speaks encouragingly to his partner, a young man from Ravenna who is new to the galley.

Going to Meet the Sultan

As for those who disbelieve,
their deeds are like a mirage in the desert
which the thirsty takes for water
til he reaches it to find that there was nothing.

—AL-QUR'ĀN

Just as Francesco prophesied, the soldiers of Christ lie dead and dying on the field of battle, and in their camp as well, for those not hacked to death by the swords of the infidel are laid low by a plague as relentless as the hot desert wind. The Nile has flooded the canal the soldiers dug to give them passage to Damietta's gates; their camp is a swamp where bright snakes and frogs dart merrily, indifferent to the groans of those abandoned by God. The knights have gone to the cardinal on their knees to ask why God should bring them to this place he has forsaken so that they might die rotting in the sun. Are there not graves enough in lands that revere his name?

Francesco and Illuminato walk among the wounded and the sick, who call out to them from pallets in the mud. The dark towers of Damietta brood over the scene, and in the evenings when the muezzins call their faithful to their unholy prayers, their shrill cry makes the wounded shield their eyes, imagining they hear the screams of carrion birds gathering over their heads.

When the friars first arrived at the camp, Cardinal Pelagius was confident of a victory. He ignored Francesco's dream of ill omen and refused him permission to attempt the conversion of the sultan. The time was propitious: the sultan had retreated from al-Adiliya, and his days, as the word of God promised, were numbered, for the false prophet of Islam had reigned 666 years, fulfilling the true prophecy of days numbered to the beast of the apocalypse. But now, faced with the defeat of Christ's army, by Saracen sword and by God's mysterious will, the cardinal has agreed to let Francesco do what he has done everywhere he goes—bring the mighty, the indifferent, the proud, the heretical, into the loving embrace of Christ's church.

A company of pilgrims and soldiers join the friars for the walk to the town of al-Adiliya, which Sultan al-Kamil has abandoned and the armies signed by the cross now occupy, cutting him off from Damietta on two sides. Therein had lain their hope of victory. The soldiers are quarrelsome; the French blame the Italians, who turned and fled in the heat of the battle; the Italians blame the cardinal, who led them into a trap; everyone blames Duke Leopold of Austria, who has returned to his own country, and before him the king of Hungary, who came out only to collect holy relics and—when he had bought or stolen the heads of St. Stephen and St. Margaret, the hands of St. Thomas and St. Bartholomew, and his greatest treasure, the rod of Aaron—packed up his ships and sailed for home.

Francesco is eager but silent. He walks out ahead of the group, kicking up dust; where the river has not moistened it, the earth is baked and dry. The sun streams down; the air rakes his throat and eyes. The bickering of the soldiers, the complaints of the women, the bitterness against him for telling his dream, the promise of martyrdom at the hands of the sultan, all draw his thoughts away from this world. Illuminato joins him. "When the sultan is converted," he says hopefully, "all his people will follow him." Francesco nods. He knows his text; his French has improved since his arrival at the camp, though he has heard more complaining than conversation.

When they arrive at the town, they are welcomed by the Knights of the Temple, who encourage the friars to rest before continuing on alone. The road is dangerous. Outside Fariskur they will be stopped by guards who will not understand them. It is possible that they will be murdered then, before they see the sultan. The friars listen attentively. Francesco takes a drink of tepid water, Illuminato tucks a piece of bread into his sleeve, and they are off. They have only a few miles to walk. For a time they see nothing but sand and stone, then Illuminato spots two sheep grazing in a thin green strip near a ditch. "Listen, Illuminato," Francesco observes, "God sends us forth like sheep in the midst of wolves. Put your trust in him." He begins the Shepherd's Psalm, and Illuminato joins him, giving the antiphon.

So they continue as if they were walking in the valley of Mount Subasio on their way to the Portiuncula, and not in this actual valley of death, fearing no evil, but relying on the guidance of their Shepherd. There is a wider stretch of green, and then, shimmering in the heat, they see the sand-colored walls of the town, surmounted by a number of thin towers which look like steam rising from a boiling cauldron. Francesco spots the guards, some on horseback, others standing at attention with their curved swords held across their chests, and then the guards see the friars. In the next moment the riders spur their horses and the foot soldiers cry out, rushing after them, waving their swords. The friars press on, bravely reciting their psalm until the thunder of hooves and shouting drowns them out. A guard leaps from his horse, knocking Francesco to his knees, and when Illuminato tries to come to his aid, he is smashed to the ground by two others, who beat him with wooden batons from their horses' backs. "Sultan," Francesco cries out. "Sultan." The foot soldiers run up, panting and furious, and pitch into the fray. One kicks Francesco in the back, another pulls him up by the shoulders and slams him down to the ground. He covers his face with his hands. "Sultan, Sultan," he pleads. When he hears Illuminato, struggling behind him in the dirt, sing out, "My cup runneth over," he laughs.

This laugh confounds the guards. These ragged, dirty men may be demons. Their captain shouts a command, and the friars are pulled to their feet. They stand dusting themselves off, submitting to the chain the guards produce to tie them together at the wrists. There are more gruff, impenetrable orders. The captain turns his horse's head back toward the town, and the foot guards, pushing the friars along with the tips of their swords, fall into step behind him. Francesco looks back at Illuminato, who pulls down the corners of his mouth, raising his eyebrows at the same time. Again, to the chagrin of his captors, Francesco laughs.

As they march toward the gates, the captain signals to a guard who stands watching from one of the towers. He shouts down into the court, there are answering shouts, and then they hear the creaking of the hinges as the gate is pulled open, revealing a small man dressed in odd raiment: half vestment, half Saracen dress, with red breeches that balloon out from beneath his alb and are tucked into soft white leather boots laced halfway to his knees. Is he a Christian, or has he only eaten one? Francesco stumbles forward, pulling Illuminato along behind him, and says, first in Italian, then in French, "I am Brother Francesco, I wish to speak to the sultan." The man responds in French, "All men have heard of Brother Francesco. I am, or once was, Father Bernard of Lyons. I went down to Marseilles in the company of those fearless children who set out to recapture the Holy Land." Illuminato tugs at Francesco's sleeve, begging for a translation, which he readily gives. The priest bids the guards release the captives. Their harsh language is soft in his mouth, but they obey him without question. Then, taking Francesco's hands in his own, he drops to his knees and says, "Brother Francesco. Give me your blessing."

"I will gladly," Francesco says and, laying his hand upon the bowed head before him, gives his blessing, his voice solemn and assured, then raises the priest to his feet. "Tell me how you have come to this place," he says.

"I will tell you as we walk along," Father Bernard assures him, leading the way into a wide, cool court where palm trees grow up over the walls and two women hurry by, their faces hidden in scarves, their shoulders bent beneath the weight of the water buckets they carry attached to wooden yokes. The priest tells the story of his travels with the children, led by the boy-preacher Stephen, and of their departure from Vendôme, though the king had bid them to return to their homes. "But we would not," he explains. "For Christ had called these children to save his Holy Sepulchre, when kings and knights had failed. As we made our way through the towns, everywhere we were made welcome, lodged and fed, and at each town more and more children joined us, so that when we arrived at Marseilles, we numbered many thousand. There, two merchants provided us with ships, for the love of Christ, or so they said, but a few days out, a storm destroyed two ships and the rest were boarded by Saracens in league with the merchants, who traded in slaves, and so we were all captured and sold in lots. I, with my companion Father Louis, had the good fortune to be sold to the sultan al-Kamil, who is a kind master and a student of religions, and who is eager to hear the preaching of Brother Francesco, of whom he has heard interesting reports."

The friars hurry along, Francesco translating the story in bits to Illuminato, who cries "God have mercy" at each frightening turn of the tale. They have crossed the court and come to a stone doorway lined with multicolored tiles, the entrance half closed by a curtain of heavy silk the color of a robin's egg. Francesco finishes Father Bernard's story as he steps inside the curtain. The room is small, perfumed by fragrant yellow flowers which grow in pots along the walls. Cushions embroidered in strange patterns are scattered on the tile floor. Sitting upon the largest of these cushions, his back supported by a wall draped in brocade of Baghdad, his turbaned head bowed over a bowl made of amber in which he is carefully dipping a golden spoon, is the sultan al-Kamil. His nose, his cheeks, his chin are all sharply etched, as if his features had been carved with an axe. When Father Bernard addresses him, he looks up, sees the friars, and shouts out in apparent joy a message they do not understand.

Father Bernard smiles. "The sultan welcomes you poor men," he says. "And as he knows you are parched from your long walk, he insists that you try this cooling dish. It is a syrup made from lemons, cooled by the snow brought especially to him from the icy mountains of Lebanon."

A Meal in an Exotic Setting

*Acre is a port of call for all ships. It is the focus of ships
and caravans, and the meeting place of Muslim and Christian
merchants from all regions. Its roads and streets are choked
by the press of men so that it is hard to put foot to ground.
It stinks and it is filthy, being full of refuse and excrement.*

—IBN JUBAYR
Travels 1182–85

The bubbling of the fountains never stops, the scent of lemons and roses is always in the air. When a servant lifts the hanging at the outer entry, a hot streak of sunlight breaks through like a gleaming shield, but otherwise the courtyard is shady and cool. Two hunters pursue a lion pursuing a deer in the mosaic on the floor, and two bronze griffins, as big as dogs, stand guard at the base of a pink marble arch that opens upon a narrow pool, like a sparkling ribbon that runs the length of the court. Date palms in carved onyx boxes stand at the corners and in the center. Overhead, the flat, hot, uninterrupted blue of the sky presses down like the lid of a jewel box, the edges carved all round in fanciful shapes.

Brother Stefano stands beneath the arch, looking in timidly. He has been traveling for a month and has seen many strange and wonderful sights, but the fragrant tranquility of this courtyard is the most wonderful of all, for just outside its high, thick walls the streets are foul with ordure and jammed with all manner of people: Africans as black as onyx; bareheaded, clean-shaven Franks; quarreling Arabs, their heads swathed in white scarves; knights from every country, in all manner of armor; Jews dressed in the richest cloths and without the yellow badges they are required to wear at home. They mingle in the crowd with impunity, more Jews than Stefano has ever seen in his life. His head aches from the racket and stench of the street, and he clutches his temples as he steps aside to allow a servant bearing a tray laden with dishes to pass into the court. A tantalizing aroma of spices—ginger, cloves, and cumin mixed with the bloody smell of cooked meat—rises over the food. He is weak with hunger and so thirsty he longs to sink down before the pool and drink deeply, and then to cool his burning feet and eyes, but he is too close to accomplishing his mission and too anxious not to offend the residents of this place, where, he has been told, or where he thinks he has been told—for he has not understood a word anyone has said to him for several days—he will find Father Francesco.

Another servant enters from the back of the court, carrying a tray of bread which he sets down on a long stone table partially hidden behind the pillars of an arch. As he turns to leave, he sees the friar and approaches him, pouring out a flood of harsh language and waving his hand as if to shoo off an unwelcome animal. Stefano steps back into the shadowy entryway. The heavy curtain parts, and a lively party of men, all speaking excitedly, bursts through. With relief, he recognizes the language as his own, and in the next moment he hears his own name called out and steps forward to greet Brother Pietro Catani, whom he has not seen in over a year. The servant has moved aside, and Stefano, absorbed at once into the group, passes him without a glance. He takes the hand of the famous brother Elia, who welcomes him cordially, inviting him to dine with them, as he must be hungry and thirsty and there is always a place for a friar at his table. Behind him a knight shouts out some pleasantry about the friars—the whole world is their dining table, in his opinion. Stefano studies him, smiling hesitantly. He has seen a good many knights in his travels, many, like this one, with the cross of the crusader sewed on their tunic, and the two-edged sword of God's vengeance ever ready at his side. They are not, like the friars, constrained to a particular greeting or manner of living; their fellowship is of a mettlesome stamp, and they defer to one another with the recondite and hierarchical ritual of wolves. Like wolves, they are volatile and dangerous, especially when separated from the pack, for they respect none but their own kind, and their voracious appetites cannot be satisfied. Stefano is careful to put Elia between himself and this red-faced, agitated knight. Behind him, two clerics, mumbling in

French, their heads bowed together, suddenly break into high-pitched laughter.

As the group approaches the table, more servants appear, bearing platters of meats, bowls of bright fruits, and enameled bronze ewers with spouts in the shape of rooster heads. Stefano glances about furtively, for he does not wish to appear as astonished as he feels. The table is low, with cushions around it for sitting, and it is covered in a dark blue silk shot with gold; the trenchers are made of hammered silver, and each place has a translucent bone spoon, a drinking bowl of polished sardonyx, and a glass phial of water. Brother Pietro takes Stefano's arm and leads him to the seat next to Elia, who is pouring water into the wine in his bowl. Before he is even seated, the knight draws his short knife and stabs a roasted bird on the nearest platter. Pietro asks Stefano about his travels, did he sail from Ancona or Brindisi, was the weather bad, and what was the news from Italia? How does the brotherhood thrive and grow, has word of the five friars martyred in Morocco reached the peaceful sanctuary of the Portiuncula? Stefano takes his seat and helps himself to the bread and a tentative swallow of wine. Pietro produces a knife from his sleeve and spears a few pieces of stewed meat, which he deposits on his friend's trencher. "Elia has taught the cook here to season the meat as we do at home," he explains. Elia smiles blandly, helping himself to the same platter. There is something reptilian about him; his eyes are slits, his full lips are too dark, almost purple, and his black beard is trimmed into a hard-edged rectangle. His smile hardly shows his teeth. "What news do you bring us, Brother Stefano?" he inquires. "Have you come as a messenger or as a pilgrim?"

"If you're heading for Jerusalem," the knight puts in, "you may as well give up and stay here. There's nothing there but ghosts and ruins, I can vouch for that."

Stefano brushes the crumbs from his beard; the bread is crumbly, not easy to eat. "I've been sent," he explains, "with a message for Father Francesco, if he is still alive."

Elia blinks, chewing thoughtfully. Then, lifting his chin toward the entry, he says, "He is here." Stefano leans back to look past Pietro's shoulder, and there, framed by the arches, is Francesco.

He has come in soundlessly and stands perfectly still, as if to admire the diners before he joins them. One by one they fall silent. The only sounds are the plash of the water in the fountains and the click of the knight's knife as he lays it down upon the table.

Brother Stefano rises to his knees, but he holds back his impulse, which is to run to this solitary figure and kneel at his feet. Francesco's eyes move from face to face, and when at last they meet Stefano's, his expression brightens with recognition. "Brother Stefano," he says, advancing toward the group, breaking the spell his presence has momentarily cast upon them, "God give you peace."

He has been preaching at the market, without, he confesses, much success, though Elia points out that he has raided the Episcopate in Acre and sent back half the staff to Assisi, eager to take the vows of the Minores, much to the chagrin of Bishop Vitry. Francesco nods, accepting a piece of bread from Elia and picking out a ripe Damascus plum and a few cherries from the platter heaped with fruit. The talk turns to Brother Stefano's travels and to the message he has brought.

Stefano pulls a much folded and sweated-upon page of parchment from his tunic; the new Rules, he explains, which the ministers Gregorio and Matteo of Narni have instituted at the Pentecost Chapter of the friars. This occasion was one of bickering and confusion; Stefano was there, and he heard acrimonious exchanges between brothers and witnessed outbursts of anger and calumny that shamed the very name of the Minores and would have shocked their blessed father, if only he had been there to instruct these obstinate and wayward friars. So Stefano's message is simply this: Father Francesco is desperately required at home and must leave at once to save the order from destruction at the hands of obstinate friars who are more in love with books than Lady Poverty.

Francesco and Pietro examine the document while Elia looks on, biting a fig. The knight is absorbed in drinking as much wine as possible, and the two clerics continue their conversation in French. The decree contains a list of new meatless days; they are, Pietro observes, in the midst of one as they sit. Francesco looks up from the writing. "What are we to do?" he asks.

"It is up to you, Father," Pietro assures him, "to say what we may or may not eat." Their eyes meet, and Francesco raises his brows at this remark, his expression suffused with amusement. Stefano sits quietly, holding his breath.

Father Bernard had been right. The sultan was kind, the sultan was attentive, but the sultan was not converted. When Francesco offered to stand in a fire to prove his was the true faith, al-Kamil expressed dismay that such a course would even be contemplated. "No, no, Brother Francesco," he exclaimed. "Surely your God does not require this." Instead, Brother Bernard explained, the sultan wished the friar to preach a sermon on the virtues of his faith.

And so the friar preached, halting every few words for Father Bernard's translation. Francesco was accustomed to letting the Holy Spirit shine through his discourse, directing the ebb and flow of his argument as the moon does the waves, but the constant interruptions divided his attention between his auditor and his inspiration. He struggled bravely on. Illuminato sat on the floor beside him, nodding approval and smiling. The sultan leaned forward on his cushion, his black eyes riveted upon Francesco, his head tilted toward Father Bernard to take in his translation. Now and then he exclaimed in what appeared to be pleasure. Francesco spoke of Christ's poverty, of his suffering, his cruel death and miraculous resurrection, of the debt that cannot be paid, and the promise of the next world where those who have served him, accepting the scorn of the world, will be united with him in ever-lasting life. At the conclusion, the sultan got up off his cushion and embraced Francesco while Father Bernard approached, repeating, "Beautiful, he says, a beautiful story." Then the sultan called his servants, made the friars sit on cushions beside him, and offered them food and drink, which they accepted readily, and gifts, which, Francesco explained, they could not take. At least, the sultan insisted, take this ring, or this cushion, or this gold plate, or this horn, or this rug, which you may use when you pray.

In the end they took the horn. Francesco promised he would use it to summon the faithful to his sermons. They bid farewell to the sultan and followed Father Bernard back to the gates, where they were put into the care of two guards who had orders to see them safely back to al-Adiliya. There they found Bishop Vitry rushing about excitedly with the news that the sultan had sent a French prisoner to Damietta to offer a truce. It was rumored that he had offered to return Jerusalem to the Christians without a fight.

And this was true, but it came to nothing. The cardinal fell out with King Jean; the offer was refused; the soldiers took sides; the Roman contingent despaired of any resolution and set sail for home. When the sultan attempted to relieve Damietta by stealth, the army of Christ repelled his troops, and those not killed in the field were murdered by the Franj women as they attempted to flee past the camp. Bishop Vitry and the friars ministered to the wounded, standing aside while the soldiers cut off the heads of the enemy, gathered them into canvas slings, and rode out to dump them at the sultan's camp. Francesco's mission of peace had been a failure. The siege of Damietta went on.

Summer's heat gave way to continuous chilling rain. The plague took more lives than the enemy, but when reinforcements arrived from France, the cardinal persuaded King Jean that the time to attack was at hand. Even as these nobles laid their plans, a strange message arrived by pigeon to their tent: there did not appear to be any guards in the towers of Damietta. A scout sent out to scale the walls came back at dawn with astonishing news. What the armies of the cross had failed to do, God had done for them. The sward between the inner and outer walls of the city was piled high with dead bodies, and the stench was such that no man could enter or leave that place without dying of it.

But enter they must. The soldiers armed themselves, the bishop called the friars to him, and they marched out in a great troop straight to the gates of the city. This time they were not met, as they had been when they broke the chain across the Nile at the outermost tower, by arrows, by a rain of Greek fire like stars melting from the sky, by Saracens screaming and hurling down stones the size of pigs. Instead, they heard only the sound of their own footsteps marching past the tower, and when they stood at the gate, the stillness that greeted them was so strange and ominous that the generals huddled together, calling Bishop Vitry to their counsel, uncertain of the proper course to take.

They decided to throw up a ladder and send a dozen men over the walls to bring back a report or, if possible, to open the gates from the inside. Francesco and Illuminato joined the bishop in prayers for the safety of these men. Their voices, petitioning the heavens, seemed unnaturally loud in the eerie quiet that was like another voice, so thoroughly did it discourage all conversing. The minutes passed slowly, indeed time seemed to have stopped at the gates of Damietta, and the soldiers, unaccustomed to waiting, milled about, grumbling to one another. Then they heard the scream of metal against metal, the grinding of chains. All turned to see the outermost gate rising inch by inch, and the soldiers pushed against one another, eager for their first glimpse of the inner court of hell.

The moat was as wide as a river, but its bed was nearly dry, and in the mud the bodies were piled three deep. These were the less recently dead, so decayed that the bones of their faces protruded through the rotting flesh. As they pushed across the plank bridge, the soldiers staggered and gagged, for the stench invaded their nostrils and closed their throats with such force that the strongest knight was defenseless against it. The scouts who stood at the next gate had wrapped their shirts around their faces. The friars and the bishop went in last. Finding the enemy slain in such numbers by the hand of God, tears filled their eyes and they called on God's mercy to help them bear the sight. They pressed on, following the soldiers through the inner gate, where they found a scene to cause the very stones to weep, for here the living struggled in the embrace of the dead. In the streets, in the shops, in the houses, the dying reached out to the invaders for pity. The plague had turned their flesh black, eaten away their lips and fingertips. Francesco and Illuminato clung to each other, following the stolid back of the bishop, who had picked up a dying child and was baptizing it as he walked along. "Brothers," he said, looking over his shoulder. "Find what living children you can and bring them to me."

And this was Francesco's mission among the infidel. He went from house to house, following the soldiers, who kicked in any doors closed against them, and he gathered up the dying children. In one room he found a baby still clinging to his dead mother's breast; in another a boy of two or three chewing a piece of bread, one hand resting upon the contorted face of his father, who had died in the act of breaking off the morsel. The soldiers pulled the bodies out into the street, rounding up anyone who could stand. They shouted to one another as they moved from house to house, their horror giving way to wonder at the riches they found behind every door. If gold could save lives, no one ever would have died in this place. As Francesco carried a baby down the stone staircase, he saw a sight more terrible than the agony of the dying: two of Christ's noble knights were fighting each other for a ewer made of beaten gold. Farther on, he passed another knight intently fastening his shield to the doorway of a house, thereby claiming everything in it, gold, jewels, rich tapestries, coin, dead and dying Saracens, as his own.

In the days that followed, the dead were dragged out onto the plain. They numbered fifty thousand. As the smoke from the burning pyres turned the sky black and the ashes of the defeated clotted the nostrils of their victors, the quarrel over the spoils turned the defenders of the cross into thieves and murderers; it was not uncommon to see one knight stab another for crossing the door of his newly claimed residence.

When Bishop Vitry invited the friars to return with him to Acre, for there were living Saracens there to convert, whereas there were only Christians now in Damietta, they readily agreed. And so Francesco came to stay in Elia's comfortable house, to pass his time preaching in the marketplace, and to receive this news, that in his absence his vicars had proclaimed more meatless days and the brotherhood was desperate for his response.

Francesco reaches into the meat platter and takes out a morsel, conveying it to his lips daintily so that the juices will not run into his beard. When he has swallowed, he dabs at his mouth with his fingertips. "Then we shall do as the Gospel tells us," he says cheerfully to the attentive assembly, "and eat whatever they put in front of us."

On His Brotherhood

A Fool and His Money

*In the 12th century . . . money began to play a major role
in everyday transactions, and the word "to earn" came
into common use. Coffers and purses are mentioned more
frequently . . . archaeologists begin to find
the remains of keys.*

—PHILIPPE ARIES
A History of Private Life

All winter long, the stories about Francesco Bernardone have blanketed Assisi like the snow, and now that the snow is melting, they swirl along the gutters and pool at the doorways of the rich. He goes about in rags, carrying a staff and a bowl like a hermit, begging for food, stones, and oil. More often than not he receives clods of mud rather than bread for his dinner. The children kick him and spin him around until he falls, even the poor revile him when they hear that he has given up his birthright. When he is not roaming the streets, he is down in the valley at San Damiano, or among the lepers at the *lazaretto*, or in San Giorgio weeping his way through the mass. His mind is afflicted, he is mad, and a fool. In the evenings he walks along the streets singing, sometimes in French: courtly songs of knights and noble ladies, of Merlin and the fellowship of the Round Table, while the rain runs down his neck and the wind bends him in half.

Lord Bernardo of Quintavalle has heard the tales, borne into his fine house by the tradesmen and the cook, of this strange young man, and he remembers Francesco as he was before this transformation, a lively, amiable fellow pulling out bolts of cloth in his father's stall, or roaming the streets of an evening with his fellows, all dressed elegantly in multicolored cloaks, surcoats, fanciful hats, leggings, and silk purses stuffed with coins. Though he has heard the stories, Bernardo is not prepared for the shock when he comes across this famous lunatic one spring morning outside the Church of San Rufino. Francesco is sitting on a low wall, occupied in sewing a patch onto his miserable garment. Bernardo stands and stares until Francesco looks up, recognizes him, and greets him with the seated equivalent of a bow. "Lord Bernardo,

God give you peace," he says. He is gaunt, pale, surely he is ill. His eyes are feverish, too bright, and his ready smile has something ghostly in it, not skeletal, but not of this world. Bernardo masks his astonishment and the peculiarly warm curiosity he feels about this outcast with some ordinary greeting, followed by remarks about the weather. The winter has been long and unusually harsh, they agree. Harder for Francesco, Bernardo thinks, who has spent it on the street. He has seen beggars and penitents before, he knows that survival is possible; he has always given alms to the poor, but he has had no acquaintance among them. Francesco turns his attention back to his sewing. The priest at San Rufino has given him the loan of this excellent needle, he explains, and he is anxious to finish the job and return it to its owner.

Bernardo watches the glint of the needle moving back and forth across the scrap of undyed wool. It is light, the thread is dark, the stitches stand out like marks in a ledger, even and neat. Francesco sews well. Bernardo has no reason to linger, but he finds he doesn't wish to go; there is something agreeable about the young tailor. "Would you grant me the honor of your company at dinner this evening, Francesco?" he blurts out. The needle stops midstitch, but Francesco makes no response. Bernardo goes on, nervously. "I have a question I want to put to you, about a course of action I propose to undertake." Francesco studies him. It has been a long time since he has sat down at a rich man's table. "It is I who am honored by your invitation," he replies. "I accept most willingly."

There is a racket in a narrow alley nearby, then the miller from Foligno emerges, leading a donkey laden with sacks of grain. He is followed by a pig which bursts ahead, its hooves clattering on the stones. The pig rushes past the two men conversing in the warm sun and disappears beyond the corner of the church. "I will see you this evening," Bernardo concludes, and Francesco nods. He watches his new friend's back as he crosses the steps and strides off toward the Porta San Pietro. Then, smiling to himself, humming a

tune he learned a few days ago when he walked up from the Portiuncula in the company of a *joculatore* from Pisa, he puts the last
two stitches into his patch.

The food at Bernardo's table is refined and abundant, the wine
robust, but Francesco eats very little and thins his wine with water.
The night air is chilly; Bernardo has had a fire lit, and the smoke
hovers over the table like an interested guest before an open casement draws it out into the night. Bernardo has raised the question
alluded to at San Rufino, but he has phrased it so cautiously that it
has more the quality of a philosophical proposition than a personal inquiry. "Suppose a man," he asked, "has received many fine
gifts from a certain lord, and he has enjoyed these gifts for some
years, but finds he has no longer any need of them and wishes to be
rid of them. How should he go about disposing of these things?"

The conversation proceeding from this question has been ami-
cable and earnest, but now the two men sit quietly in a haze of contentment, and the only sound is the hiss and pop of the dying coals
in the grate. A servant appears to announce that a second bed
has been made up; Francesco has accepted his host's invitation to
stay the night.

Bernardo takes up a taper from the table and leads the way into
the darkness at the end of the room. Together the two men climb
the few wide steps to a low-ceilinged room, where an oil lamp
burns and two beds are piled with quilted coverlets and furs.
Francesco bids his host good night, steps out of his shoes, and
throws himself down on the nearer of the two beds without so
much as loosening his leather girdle. Bernardo smiles to himself as
he takes off his shoes, leggings, surcoat, and girdle, leaving only
his full linen shirt and breeches. He drapes his clothes neatly
across the bar, folds back a quilt, and slips in beneath it. He can see
Francesco's back in the dim lamplight, so still he does not seem

even to be breathing. He must be exhausted from the life he is living, and the bed has drawn him directly into the embrace of sleep.

All evening Bernardo has felt a consuming curiosity about his guest, who is so courteous, who expresses himself with such simplicity and directness and appears to be as comfortable at a fine table as he is dining in a gutter. Indeed, it is as if all the world is one to him. Bernardo's eyes wander over Francesco's shaggy head, his thin, motionless shoulders, and it comes to him that he is not sleeping. He is waiting for something. But for what? For Bernardo to sleep? He resolves to play a hoax, to close his eyes, breathe slowly and deeply, then make snoring sounds.

And he is right. After just a few snorts and bellows, which Bernardo amuses himself so much in making that he can hardly keep from laughing, he hears a rustle of cloth, the sound, he thinks, of his guest getting out of the bed. This presents a dilemma, for if he opens his eyes, he will surely be discovered, the lamp will give him away. He strains his ears to make out, between the bursts of his own fake snores, any sound in the room. At first there is nothing, and he wonders if he was mistaken in his assumption; perhaps what he heard was only Francesco turning in his sleep. Then he hears something, a deep sigh, so woeful and compelling that, without his will, his eyes fly open and he looks across the room to find Francesco standing there, his face to the wall, his hands open, palms up, his head dropped forward. Another sigh fills the chilly air, punctuated by a catch in the throat, a sob, and then the words "My God" whispered softly, his head lifted now as if to speak into an intent and listening ear.

Bernardo does not move; he scarcely breathes. The lamplight flickers in the darkness, making the shadow Francesco casts upon the wall vibrate as if it were itself a flame and the breath of these heartrending sighs made it tremble. Again the whispered plea, "My God," followed by a shuddering intake of breath, tremulous and long, like a brokenhearted child.

What depth of sadness is this? Bernardo asks himself. Tears well up in his eyes, and his vision blurs. He cannot bring himself to speak, though if he could, he knows it would be to offer useless consolation, for this humble supplication has a powerful, insistent energy that wants no comfort. So he remains still and watchful, and he listens to the sighs and groans that fill the silence of the room like some unearthly music. He can feel his own heart pounding dully in his chest, his fingertips are numb, and his breathing remains shallow. Tears course silently down his cheeks, over his ears, and into his hair. He is himself a godly man. He has sought to serve and please the Lord, he has attended faithfully to the mass, listened to the readings from the Gospels, taken communion, confessed his sins, and bowed his head in prayer, but he knows that before this night, he has been entirely untouched and unmoved by God. He is agitated, disturbed as he has not been before, and he feels that Francesco has reached into his soul and stirred some smoldering embers there so that, should he be offered even the most meager fuel, he will burst into flame. The air in the room is charged, as it is after a storm when everything stale, lifeless, ephemeral has been blown away. Bernardo lies still, and Francesco goes on, hour after hour. The intensity of his suffering does not abate; he is determined to break through every barrier, in this world or the next, that separates him from God.

Toward dawn, without knowing it, Bernardo slips into sleep. When he opens his eyes, he looks across the room to find Francesco lying on his back on the bed, his hands folded over his chest, contemplating the ceiling. He turns his head to look at Bernardo, but he does not speak. He looks tired; there are dark circles under his eyes, and the smile he gives his friend is wan.

Bernardo throws off his cover and sits up on the edge of the bed. He can still feel the warmth, the strange excitement of the night. "Listen, Francesco," he says. "I've made up my mind to leave the world and follow you. I will do whatever you order me to do."

Bernardo's house faces a small square where three streets come together, giving it the advantage of light in the upper rooms. His cook keeps pots of herbs on the window ledges—mints, rosemary, and sage for cooking; lemon balm, marjoram, lavender, and ladies' bedstraw for medicines—and on a warm damp day like this one, the pleasant scents mingle in the air so that the passersby look up to find the source of the agreeable perfumes. The cook is in the window himself, having moved one of the larger plants so that he may lean out to watch the increasingly frantic scene in the street below.

The news has traveled quickly. There can scarcely be a soul in the town who doesn't know that Bernardo is selling off the contents of his house, and at such prices one would be a fool not to buy something, even if he has no need of it. Francesco and Bernardo have hauled the heavier furnishings into the street, and the early buyers have made their offers, which have all been accepted without argument. Bernardo will not haggle. He has a sack inside his cloak which has grown heavy with coins. The new owners stand about, guarding their purchases. Young men converge on the scene pushing all manner of handcarts, and petty arguments over the price of removal flare up among the buyers, who shout at one another over their benches, tables, and chests. A troop of beggars arrives from the city gate; they have got the scent of silver. Bernardo and Francesco, to the chagrin of the crowd, commence handing out fistfuls of coins to them. To pay good silver only to see it cast upon beggars is an outrage, the butcher complains. If Lord Bernardo has no need of their money, then why can't the upright citizen enjoy the same largesse as the beggar and take the stuff without paying?

The beggars aren't satisfied either. They want to help themselves to the fine silks and dyed woolens that one of their company has discovered in a chest left unguarded in the doorway. This ragged fellow wraps a skein of blue silk around his shoulders and dances about, calling on his comrades to witness how well the color suits his complexion. A shoemaker and his assistant push past him into the house and take up a three-legged cauldron from the hearth, which they demand, for they say they have great use of it, more than a beggar has of silk. This reasoning works like a stimulant upon the crowd milling about the door. They rush inside, grabbing up whatever they can find and hold—trivets, pot-hooks, flesh-hooks, wine jugs, silver and pewter trenchers and platters, leather tankards, horn mugs and clay pitchers, cushions, and candle-stands. Though their arms are full, still they wrestle with one another for some choice bit none has the means to carry away. Two old women ease their way past the quarreling men and quietly begin taking down the gold-and-emerald-striped hanging that covers the long wall where the dining table once stood.

Bernardo and Francesco enter the fray, pleading in the name of God for some courtesy, some decorum, but they are caught up by the arms like bad children and deposited in the street. A stone-mason follows them, his shoulders draped in linen shirts, breeches, and wool leggings. In one hand he has an inkwell and a carved ivory box. He drops two coins in Bernardo's lap, then joins a carter who is struggling to carry three oil lamps and a leather tankard full of spoons. Francesco lies sprawled in the dirt, propped up on his elbows while people step over him and sometimes on him in their haste to get into the house. Bernardo calls out as he dips into his sack, distributing coins to the outstretched hands of the beggars, who have landed upon him like a pack of starving dogs— "Francesco, are you hurt?" A big, rough woman accosts him and relieves him of his cloak. The doorway is jammed with people struggling to get in and those, laden with booty, struggling to get out. There is much swearing and shouting, more often than not the loot is carried away without even a token payment, and Bernardo's pouch grows light.

Francesco gets to his feet slowly, brushing off his tunic, laughing as he is pushed this way and that by the mob, which is becoming angry now because there is so little left of value. "Brother," he says to Bernardo as he staggers to his friend, extending his hand to help him to his feet. "My dear brother Bernardo." Bernardo takes his hand and rises from the dirt, but no sooner is he standing than two men accost him and pull his doublet from his shoulders. Another rips off his money sack and, finding it empty, resorts to tearing his linen shirt from his back. Francesco watches, his eyes burning with amusement, while Bernardo shouts, "No, no, don't tear it, I will give it to you." When the man has the shirt, he runs into the house. Bernardo pats his sweating torso, grinning at Francesco. Their attention is drawn to the upper window, where the cook is shouting for help. He struggles with a man who is attempting to carry off a heavy pot of lavender. "This is not his to give away," the cook protests. "This is mine and I am not giving anything away today."

Francesco and Bernardo stand gazing up at the hopeless plight of the cook, a small, wiry man, no match for his hulking and furious opponent. The pot sways between them until, in a sudden lurch, both men lose their grip upon it. It teeters on the ledge, and the crowd, sensing danger, pushing and shouting, scatters out of its path. Then, as if making a leap for freedom, the pot slips off the ledge and, with a thunderous crash that momentarily silences the hubbub in the square, shatters on the stones below.

An Interview

A striking feature of medieval religious history is the emergence and popularity of religious rules. Why were these rules written? The early Christians were not monks.

—ROSALIND BROOKE
The Coming of the Friars

There are twelve of them living with the old priest at San Damiano, though they work most days repairing the ruined chapel at the Portiuncula. They all dress alike in plain wool tunics with a cowl and a cord at the waist. They wear no shoes and carry no purse. One of them told the baker they live according to a rule written by that crazed son of Pietro Bernardone, who has disgraced his family. They are a brotherhood, a new order, but an order of what? They aren't monks, many of them aren't clerics, they live like the poor men of Lyons, nurse the sick and the lepers like the Paterini, but they do not rail against the clergy who sell indulgences at auction, keep mistresses, and stable their sheep in the church. They come into the town two at a time, begging food, stones, mortar, and they preach repentance. They warn of the ease with which the unwary sinner is tempted by the pleasures of this world to lose all hope of the next, so that he wakes from the sleep of death to find himself hurtling headlong into hell, damned eternally to unspeakable tortures and cut off from the love of God, that love which sent the Lord Christ to live as a beggar among men, to die an outcast and a criminal so that those who love him might know the infinite joy of heaven.

A shepherd reports that he has seen Francesco and his followers on the Foligno road, walking one behind the other, loudly reciting their prayers like a line of honking gray geese. They are on their way to Roma and so completely mad that they think the Lord Pope Innocent will approve their simpleminded Rule.

These poor men, who say they are living as the apostles lived, trusting God to provide for them, homeless, wandering the earth, taking no care for the morrow, calling themselves the Penitents of

Assisi, the servants of all, living in ruined buildings abandoned by men, sleeping in nests on the ground like animals, who is to say whether they are the shame or the pride of Assisi?

They have arrived at the Palazzo Laterano, a city within the city, and made their way through the outer courts and inner vestibules to the great hall, where the Lord Pope receives the never-ending tributes and entreaties of the horde that constitutes Christ's church on earth. Clerics and prelates, secretaries and legates, lords and guildsmen, each in the costume suitable to his situation and rank, occupy themselves with the ceremonies required to command for even one moment the sublime attention of His Holiness. Bishop Guido guides Francesco and his brothers through the crowd, exchanging a word with a guard here, a secretary there, until they stand before a pair of doors as tall as trees which open before them with an impressive creaking of hinges, like the long-unopened gates of paradise. They are herded inside by the bishop and passed along by a series of papal functionaries. The Lord Pope, seated at the far end of the great room on his high stone chair, leans forward to watch their approach. The babble of conversation does not entirely cease, but the volume drops appreciably as all eyes are gradually drawn to this ragged, uncouth, unwashed collection of bumpkins, whose bare feet slap sharply on the polished marble floors. Their small, dark, bright-eyed leader steps out ahead of them, his eagerness so barely contained he seems to execute a bizarre new dance step as he charges forward. The pope sends Cardinal Giovanni, who stands at his side, an incredulous look—*this* is his discovery? This inelegant creature fresh from the sty? This is his idea of what the Church will require if it is to stem the flood of heresy and dissension that is washing down from the north? Truly, God's wonders have not ceased.

When Francesco arrives at the foot of the stairs, his progress is checked by a terse command from a guard. He looks up to

Cardinal Giovanni, who nods at him distantly. He sweeps back the skirt of his unsightly tunic as if it were the robe of an emperor and inclines his head and shoulders in a lordly bow. He can hear the cardinal's introduction: "Here is our brother Francesco di Pietro Bernardone of Assisi, whom I have examined, and who begs the ear of Your Holiness." Francesco keeps his head down but raises his eyes and looks directly into the Lord Pope's opaque and chilly scrutiny. His golden corona is studded with jewels; it rises above his head like the dome of an enormous gleaming beehive, and the rigid collar of his cope obscures the lower part of his face, so that he appears to be a small mound of gold, brocade, and jewels, from which peer steadily two heavy-lidded, skeptical gray eyes above a long, aquiline nose. As Francesco stares, uncertain whether to speak, genuflect, or back away cautiously, the folds of the cope rustle, and a small, pale hand appears, the index finger extended, pointing at him. Then the finger crooks once in a summoning gesture. Francesco casts an anxious look at the cardinal, who lifts his chin, reinforcing the pope's command. Eagerly, Francesco climbs the wide stone steps that bring him to the foot of the papal throne.

The brothers stay behind, pressed together in a nervous clutch, too intimidated to follow their master. Various prelates, guards in light armor, messengers in short coats and red leggings move around them; others seated on the long stone benches that flank the tapestry-draped walls fill the air with interminable chat. A bishop, wrapped in a heavy green silk mantle, leaning on a crook with a miniature ivory cathedral at the top, carries an embroidered pillow, which he plumps up before taking a seat upon it. The air is still, cold, and the smoke from the censers rises continually, banking in a thick cloud against the coffered ceiling.

Francesco stands before the Lord Pope, nodding his head at something the cardinal is saying. Pope Innocent listens, his neck bent forward beneath the weight of his corona, his shoulders drooped beneath the weight of his robes. His gaze wanders from the cardinal to Francesco, then out to the friars, huddled together nervously like sheep liable to panic and run off a cliff if their shepherd isn't quick about his business. Innocent looks back at the shepherd in question, a dreamy fellow at best, full of enthusiasm, lacking judgment, doubtless barely literate, though Bishop Guido and Cardinal Giovanni have assured His Holiness that these penitents do much good in their district, nursing the poor and even the lepers, repairing churches, preaching repentance and, more importantly, respect for the Holy See. How much harm could they do if sanctioned, and how much more if refused? He presses his eyelids with his fingertips, listening to the cardinal, who seems determined to keep his protégé from ever speaking for himself.

The brothers have begun to feel more at ease and look about curiously. Brother Egidio, gazing up into the gloom, makes a discovery which he brings to the attention of Brother Angelo. Up there, on the capital of that column, can he see it? Angelo cranes his neck; he doesn't see anything. Then, as Egidio raises his arm to point, Angelo does see it. But what is it? Is it a sparrow or a wren? The bird hops from one marble leaf to another, then takes off in the direction of the doors. It is a sparrow. They follow its dizzy flight as it sails through the cloudy upper atmosphere of the room.

"It seems to me your way of life is too hard," the pope comments at last, addressing himself pointedly to Francesco, who smiles as if he expected just this objection, though he says not a word to refute it. Straightaway the cardinal offers his unsolicited opinion, which is that it might cause painful and unnecessary misunderstandings among the laity if the Holy Father should decree that the way of life recommended in the Gospels is too difficult for a Christian to undertake. This is not, the pope concedes, an insignificant point. And as he considers it, his gaze wanders again out to the friars huddled there in the aisle; surely an unpromising lot. Look, one of them is rubbing his eyes with two fists like a sleepy child, and two others stand apart, gazing up at the ceiling, their mouths ajar like two simpletons standing in a field and making fantastic pictures out of the clouds.

A Convocation of Friars

*A genuine first-hand religious experience . . . is bound to be
a heterodoxy to its witnesses, the prophet appearing as a
mere lonely madman. If his doctrine proves contagious
enough to spread to any others, it becomes a definite and
labeled heresy. But if it then still prove contagious enough
to triumph over persecution, it becomes itself an orthodoxy;
and when a religion has become an orthodoxy, its day of
inwardness is over: the spring is dry; the faithful live at
second hand exclusively and stone the prophets in their turn.*

—WILLIAM JAMES
The Varieties of Religious Experience

Like locusts the rumors swarmed down into Umbria from the north, and everywhere the friars lifted their heads, they heard the incessant grinding of jaws. Francesco has not died in the east, he has come back. He has arrived in Venezia, he is ill and forced to rest there, but he has heard of the trouble at the last Chapter and he has returned to settle it. Then he has recovered his health, he is in Bologna. There has been a fearful confrontation at the House of Studies and he has forced even the sick and dying friars into the street. Now he has left Borgo San Sepolcro, he is on his way to the Portiuncula, and a new chapter has been called.

After the rumors came the friars, pouring in from every region. These were not the singing, carefree beggars of the early days but a legion of humorless administrators, the provincial ministers, and every one, it seemed, came with his own particular grievance. They filled the narrow plain, turning the resident friars out of their huts, arguing and complaining about everything, but especially about one another. The Commune of Assisi provided a house for them and sent down dozens of hampers full of bread and eggs, all quickly consumed. The Paris contingent clamored for cheese while the friars from Le Marche mocked them and suggested they would next require pheasants and larks roasted on a spit.

A messenger arrived; Francesco was near. He had stopped at Citta di Castello. Brothers Elia and Pietro Catani followed the messenger, having walked without stopping from Venezia. They were received with an ostentatious display by Bishop Guido, who confessed himself overcome by the honor of offering hospitality to the second in command of this sprawling, bickering army of

God. He brought out the best of his wines, nagged his cook to tears, and the three religious ate and drank late into the night. In the morning the two friars took communion from their host and went out into the sunny square, where another messenger rushed up with the news that Francesco had arrived.

If he can't leave the friars and carry the Gospel to the infidel without coming back to find his brothers squabbling, setting up schools, and living in stone houses, what will become of them when he is dead and cannot be called back? Francesco has been walking for days, but he is not tired. Everywhere he goes, he hears discouraging stories, tales of friars who study books and seek to be admired for their learning, who wear new cloth and sit with women, who even eat from the same bowl as women, of friars seeking special favors from the pope, of friars living in the houses of the rich as faithful retainers, of a brother who is traveling about the countryside with a group of lepers, men and women together, all wearing the gray tunic of the Fratres Minores.

At Venezia, on the little island where he had found a refuge, Francesco listened all night to the sea battering the shore, and he gazed out into the blackness laid against the black water, forming a seam he could discern only when the waves folded over white against it. Premonitions visited him like ravens, alighting on his shoulders, flapping their powerful wings and croaking as he paced the marshy shoreline with his arms crossed over his chest to hold in the racing of his heart. If the friars defied him at the chapter, as Elia told him they intended to do, how could he, who was bound by holy obedience to be the servant of all, instruct them with anything other than the example of his entire submission?

Now he is walking quickly on the road he knows better than any other, past the high walls of Assisi, past the *lazaretto* where two men, one without a nose, the other with lips that are split by a festering gash from nose to chin, look up from a quarrel they are having and rush after him, ringing their clappers and shouting for alms. Francesco stops to let them catch up, but they have lost interest already and returned to their argument. He turns off the road, down through the grove of ilex to the clearing of the Portiuncula.

There are chattering groups of friars scattered everywhere, near the rough portico of the chapel, and among the wattled huts. Some of them pause to watch him as he passes but do not recognize him. For his part, he has lost sight of everything but a low stone building that stands near the rail fence bordering an orchard. In the open doorway of this edifice, two friars are absorbed in conversation, heedless of the approaching stranger who gesticulates excitedly and mutters something that is surely not a prayer. As he rushes past them toward the wall where a ladder has been left leaning up into the trees, these friars notice him at last and their eyes follow him curiously. One presses his lips together tightly, while the other opens his eyes wide and says, "It is Father Francesco."

Francesco wrestles the ladder away from the wall and drags it across the dusty yard, dispersing a congregation of outraged chickens, up to the building where he rights it with a thud against the overhang of the roof. All around, the friars repeat, "It is Francesco" and move toward the house. Those who have never seen him consult with those who have, and these express surprise at how changed he is, how small and ill he looks, though he is certainly animated and quick, for before they are all near enough to see him, he has scrambled up the ladder and begun prying at the tiles near the top of the roof. Now the friars repeat to one another what one of them claims he heard their father muttering as he passed among them: "We do not live in *houses*. We do not live in *houses*."

The first tile flies down with a loud crack as it hits the hard ground; a friar dodges a second as it comes crashing near his feet. The sun pours down over Francesco, the anti-carpenter, crouched on the hot roof, bent to the work. As he pries each tile free, he flings it behind him without looking to see where it will land. The friars back away in horrified amazement, and the tiles rain down in every direction, as if it were a whirlwind and not this small and furious man who glares down upon them, his eyes hot, his teeth bared in a fierce smile, sweat pouring over his brow. With energy and joy he pulls up and smashes the hard, cold evidence that his bright dream has ended.

It is the hour of prime, and the friars are gathered on the field, their hands, eyes, and voices raised in the hazy morning light. The birds rustle in every tree and bush, the cooing of doves makes a delicate antiphon to the swell and fall of their mellifluous chanting, and the world is bathed in a heady effluvium of light and sound. It is as if nothing has changed, there is nothing to fear, and this army Francesco has raised is the pride of heaven.

He stands in their midst, singing with all his strength. *O God, the haughty have risen up against me, and the company of fierce men seeks my life.* Though he is small, his voice is big, and the sound of it, the feel of it pouring out over his lips, seems to lift him off the ground, as if he throws out a golden cord that will catch on some celestial balcony and draw him up, away from petty squabbles and jealousies, away from these brothers, these children who will not love one another unless they have a law to protect them from one another.

Like children, though they call him Father, they want to be free of him; they want their inheritance. Many of them are educated; he is unlettered; they think him a fool. The Portiuncula has been buzzing with the story of how he behaved at the house, and especially of how meekly he gave in when the bishop told him he was destroying the property of the Commune, which was a gift to the friars, though not owned by them, a kind of permanent interest-free loan. And there was much talk of how, when he learned that the schoolhouse in Bologna, which he had ordered closed and destroyed, was already reopened, Francesco had cursed Pietro Staccia, and how later, when news came that this minister had fallen ill and was near death, Francesco had refused to soften his condemnation. "Our Blessed Lord Jesus Christ has confirmed in heaven that curse which I laid on him," he snapped, "and he is accursed!"

At the first chapter meeting, he was taciturn and petulant when replying to the cases put before him, and there were many, of the difficulties attendant on managing the far-flung ministry without recourse to a more precise rule as well as some reliable source of funding: "the more the friars turn away from poverty, the more the world will turn away from them." Now he stands before them singing, his hands open at his sides, his eyelids slightly parted so that the whites are visible, like a man in a trance—*I am a man without strength. My couch is among the dead*—and all around him, the friars sing too. Some have their eyes closed, but others, open-eyed, stare curiously, suspiciously, resolutely, at Francesco, and they seem to see right through him to the problem he represents.

When the morning service is over, they all sit down where they have been standing and the whispering begins. Francesco and Pietro Catani are seated together. Elia, who has just arrived, joins them, but they do not speak. An argument has broken out between two friars, neither of whom Francesco recognizes; so many of his brothers are strangers now. Their disagreement is taken up by others who sit about in small defensive groups like so many garrisoned towns firing sheets of arrows in all directions at once. The question is whether, when they travel, they should not be allowed to carry anything. The present Rule forbids it, on this they do agree, but shouldn't an exception be made for holy books? Shouldn't a friar who is called to preach the Word of Christ at any time, in any land, carry that precious Word with him?

Francesco listens, his eyes lowered, a diffident smile fixed on his lips, the expression of a man who is doing his best to tolerate an insistent toothache. Sooner or later they will turn to him for an answer, and he knows that no answer will satisfy them all. Can he find one that will satisfy none of them?

The problem, Brother Antoine of the Parisian contingent complains, is the Rule. "It is too general and simpleminded, and it is unclear." A murmur of agreement goes up. A wild-eyed young man with a well-tended beard and the smallest tonsure Francesco has ever seen stands up and points at him, calls him "Father," and urges him to end this dispute, to give them a solution that takes into account the needs of those who are educated and understand the importance of learning. Even the accusing finger, Francesco notes, is clean and shapely, the nail trimmed and filed into a perfect crescent.

Francesco raises his hand and dabs at his right eye with the sleeve of his tunic. Then, taking in a long breath, he looks from one group to the next, staring into the impatient, serious, bitter faces, and as he does, they look back at him one by one, silent and subdued, as if his gaze, so full of sadness yet so free of reproach, had some miraculous power. Slowly he draws his robe in around his ankles, presses one hand against the ground and rises to his feet. He is no longer the wiry dynamo who tried to take down a building with his bare hands, or even the transfixed singer who stood among them moments ago. Now he is only a beggar, poor and ill, a man who has been traveling for far too long and is in desperate need of sleep. "From henceforth," he says, opening his hands before him to indicate the immensity of the time he has in mind, "I am as one who is dead to you."

In the pause that follows, the only sound is the rush of air moving into several hundred gasping throats. The young man drops his hand to his side and looks about uncertainly—this is not an answer he can make any use of.

"But here is Brother Pietro Catani," Francesco continues, and he reaches out to his old friend, raising him to his feet like a suitor leading his lady into a dance, "whom I and all of you shall obey." One of the brothers of Le Marche cries out, "Francesco, no," and

Elia, who sits at Francesco's bare feet rubbing his lower lip between his thumb and forefinger, does not succeed in holding back a low groan of disbelief. Francesco is kneeling before Pietro; he presses his forehead against the bare toes of his successor. Pietro bends over him. "Francesco," he says. "Please, get up."

Francesco does not get up. He embraces Pietro's ankles and vows that he will, in all things, obey him, but he does not obey him, for he does not get up. Instead, the others rise to their feet all across the field, some protesting, some frankly weeping. "Our father abandons us," one exclaims, and his neighbor, taking up the image, cries out, "Now we are orphans."

At the far edge of the field, Bishop Guido looks on, adjusting the folds of his pallium, his face, in the reddish shade of his wide-brimmed hat, preoccupied and gloomy. No one knows better than he the impossibility of changing Francesco's mind once it is made up.

The friars crowd around Francesco, bitterly reproaching him. How can he desert them? they cry. How can they go out into the world if their father refuses to give them guidance? What will become of them, what will become of the order, what are they to say when they return to their provincial chapters?

Francesco does not reply. His kneeling before them is his answer, and it is the only answer they will ever get.

Innocent Calls the Faithful

For even if Rome falls into complete ruin, yet nothing that is intact can be compared to it. As has been said,
Nothing can equal Rome, Rome even in ruins:
Your ruins themselves speak loud your former greatness. The ruin of Rome shows clearly, I think, that all temporal things are near their end, when the centre of all worldly things, Rome, daily languishes and decays.
—Master Gregory's Book on the Marvels
Which Were Once at Rome or Are Still There

The crows are knee-deep on the Flaminian Way, and Francesco is forced to wade through them; their congregation is not much disturbed by his presence. Reluctantly, they part ranks to let him pass. A few take advantage of the opportunity to peck at his ankles or to tear a few threads from the hem of his robe. They make a great and continuous clamor, clacking their sharp beaks and rolling their heads up toward him, their eyes gleaming like polished black stones. They are bad omens. Some say the spirits of murderers and suicides live in them, like the spirit of the emperor Nero, who, through the agency of these birds, created such a racket in the walnut tree over his grave that the outraged pope had the tree cut down, burned, and thrown into the Tevere. In its place he built a chapel to the Holy Virgin. So the old emperor was silenced, but the strutting crows still pave the road to Roma, indifferent to the progress of popes and emperors, or barefoot friars who come down from Umbria to attend the great council at the Palazzo Laterano. For days now the roads in all directions have been thick with crows and clergy.

Francesco has been to this city before, and he knows his way to the cardinal's house, where he has been invited to stay while the council is in session. The rumor is that the Lord Pope will forbid the creation of new orders, and there is some talk that the Fratres Minores, who have no Rule that has been approved by more than a nod of the papal tiara, will be forced to accept some older form, the Augustinian or the Benedictine. Francesco has little anxiety about this matter. There are now, as he has himself observed, too many Fratres Minores, and the pope has given his consent, if not in writing then at least in public, to their noble enterprise.

Francesco has come to Roma because he is curious to see this great assembly called from so many distant lands: bishops, archbishops, abbots, ambassadors, and legates from every sovereign, from cold lands to the north and from the east as far as Constantinople and Acre. The Lord Pope Innocent, it is more than rumored, will decree a great truce among all Christian nations so that they may unite in preparation for a mighty crusade to reclaim the Holy Sepulchre from the infamy of Saracen captivity. Francesco dreams of joining such a crusade, not as a knight but as a friar, preaching repentance. The air is raw and damp. Towering clouds roll swiftly toward the city as if they too have been called to attend the council. At the gates Francesco stops to speak to a group of rough men, thieves, no doubt, who grumble unintelligibly at his blessing. Farther on, as he turns away from the city walls, he passes a spacious residence with a wide loggia across the front, fig trees at one side, and a small vineyard at the back. A handsome brick tower is attached by a low crenellated wall, giving it the look of a comfortable, airy fortress.

The fall rains have washed mud into the road, and grasses grow thick among the ancient stones. There are scrubby bushes, a few pines and cypress, and various ruins, the remains of what must have been grand buildings, now reduced to heaps of rubble. Francesco stops to watch two men trying to pull out a block of marble by harnessing it to a horse. They are impatient, shouting at each other in accents so thick Francesco can only make out a word here or there, but he observes that they have wrapped the stone securely, their ramp and wagon are sturdy, and the horse, in spite of his owner's agitation, appears calm and willing. They will succeed.

He walks on, tired now and thirsty, but Roma is near and no one is thirsty there for long, even the beggars, for the water still pours in from the imperial aqueducts, through the fabulous network of pipes and into a hundred pools and makeshift fountains. When he climbs a last green hill, he will see the forest of towers, then descend into the frenzy of the city, where the Romans carry on their daily routines, as fractious and excitable as the crows on the road, reluctant to give way and eager to rob and cheat all outsiders. But they have taken to this council with enthusiasm; the whole world is coming to Roma to be fleeced. The celebration will be greater than the crowning of an emperor, without the usual riots, for the Commune has rallied behind the pope, and though the emperor will be conspicuously absent, even he will be forced to acknowledge that Christ's authority has its seat here, in Roma.

At the top of the hill, Francesco pauses to look down upon the scene. Bright banners fly from every tower, whole buildings are draped in billowing cloth. Briskly he descends, and soon he is caught up in the crowd winding through the streets, an endless and colorful procession of pilgrims, jongleurs, merchants, clerics, abbots, bishops and archbishops, knights, and lords in all manner of dress, sporting every sort of headgear, feathered, wide-brimmed in red and black, tall miters embroidered in gold, jeweled caps and crowns, gleaming helmets. Prelates brandishing copper, gilt, and enameled croziers, penitents struggling beneath black crosses as tall as buildings, horses richly caparisoned in red, purple, blue, and yellow, wagons loaded with everything from chairs to squawking chickens, all throng past the golden flanks of the emperor Constantine's horse to the palace of San Giovanni in Laterano, there to assist the Lord Pope Innocent in the reform of Christ's church and the spread throughout the world of the greater glory of God.

A Funeral, Sparsely Attended

There is no one who dies as solitary and forsaken as a pope.

—THOMAS OF ECCLESTON
Tractatus de Adventu Fratrum Minorum ad Angliam

Perugia's walls rise high and dark above the streets where two friars walk one behind the other, with heads lowered and faces hidden in their cowls. They cross an alley and come into a piazza where the houses are shuttered and blank like sleeping faces. An iron cage is attached to a bare section of wall by iron hinges embedded in the stone, and in this cage a man, naked but for a thin cloth covering his loins, lies still, barely breathing. The friars pass him at a distance. His fingers clasp the bars of his prison and his feverish eyes follow them, but he does not speak. They duck into a covered passageway and disappear into the darkness.

All his life, from the secure perch of his own hilltop city, Francesco has looked across the valley at this one, and all his life he has hated it. He has fought against its soldiers, tasted defeat and capture on its fields, and spent a full year of his youth languishing in its hellish jail. Later, when he lay down his arms and took up the cross, he came here, as he goes everywhere, preaching repentance and found neither converts nor ordinary civility, so he stood in the town square and cursed the stiff-necked citizens for their pride and their ceaseless quarreling.

But there is no escaping this place, or so it seems, nor the problem it presents, for the Commune of Assisi is in league with the emperor, and Perugia, the perennial enemy of Assisi, has sworn its allegiance, as has Francesco, to the pope.

Therefore, when the Lord Pope Innocent decided to intervene in a dispute between the cities of Pisa and Genoa which hindered the progress of his proposed Crusade, he moved his household and his cardinals north to his residence here, in Perugia. This action surprised no one, but what has brought Francesco and Leone in haste from the Portiuncula is an event that must astonish and alter the world, for no sooner had Christ's vicar settled in his temporary quarters than he was struck by a sudden illness, and, before his doctors could agree upon a course of treatment, he was dead.

The two friars emerge from the passageway into a large piazza, and there is the cathedral. The heavy portals stand open above the wide stone staircase, as if it were a feast day and a crowd were expected, though there is not a living soul in the square. Indeed, the stillness of the place is so eerie and unexpected that the friars pause and regard each another silently; then Francesco goes ahead, hurrying up the steps and through the doorway. He stops just inside, and Leone draws up beside him. Together they peer into the dolorous gloom of the nave. An acrid scent assails their nostrils, not incense but rotting flesh, and as their eyes adjust to the darkness, they discover the source of this nauseating odor: a dead man, covered only in a short, torn linen tunic, lies in a heap upon a low marble slab before the choir gate, as if dropped there from the high coffered ceiling.

"*Dio,*" Leone exclaims softly, receiving a look that is both disapproving and complicitous from Francesco, who takes a few steps forward. "Is it really the Lord Pope?" he asks.

Cautiously, the two go forward among the ancient columns, as if approaching through a forest. Is it possible? Is this the same Lord of the Church who called thousands of the faithful to Roma only a few months ago, who stood before them in his rich robes, his golden crown, who raised his golden staff to call through this delegation on all of Christendom to prepare a righteous war against the infidel? The friars stand mute before the naked corpse. His face is turned toward them, his mouth frozen open in a grimace of fear, the upper lip pulled back over long, equine teeth; his eyes are open, staring down at his own outstretched, ringless fingers. He is the realization of the truth they preach wherever they go, that the riches of this earth are as nothing, that the mighty approach the throne of God in the same condition as the poorest beggar, clothed in nothing but their sins. Leone steps back, covering his nose with his hand: Francesco reaches out and takes the dead hand in his own.

On the Poor Ladies

An Escape by Torchlight

*Puritans who lived in monastic isolation themselves, the
[church] Fathers were inclined by experience to anti-feminism,
and faced with the paradox of exalted Christian women
and debased Roman ones, they hit on what was to become
an enduring formula: they loved virgins but hated women.
"Per mulierem culpa successit, per virginem salus evenit,"
they wrote—"sin came through a woman, but salvation
through a virgin."*

—CARROLY ERICKSON
The Medieval Vision

If her desire had been to live in idle comfort among the wealthy ladies of the Benedictines, she would have gone to them at the proper hour, attired as a novice and with her mother's blessing, not, as she did, in the dead of night, dressed in a rough tunic, her hair freshly shorn, spirited through the forest by three boisterous young men who waved their torches in time to their singing to frighten, so they said, all beasts, thieves, or devils who might block their progress. Pacifica, who had been persuaded to join Chiara only after days of tearful pleading and cajoling, cast her a conspiratorial smile as they rushed through the dark woods, their arms laced together—how often had they traipsed about the town this way. Chiara felt her heart throbbing with the joy of the escape, and the wide prospect of liberty. She would have no husband on this earth. Francesco, her friend, her lord and liberator, danced ahead of her on the path, singing to them of the favors they would receive for bringing Lady Chiara to be the bride of the Holy Spirit, and the handmaiden of their patroness, Lady Poverty. He turned, bowing to Chiara in the midst of his clownish dance, and Leone and her cousin Rufino followed his lead, circling the young ladies with elaborate obeisances. She threw her head back—how light it felt without the burden of her hair—and raised her arms to the moon shining down through the trees, giddy with the madness of it, the freedom of it. She recalled the supernatural strength that had come to her aid when, struggling with the bar on her father's door—the door that opened only when someone died—she had thrown her weight against it and lifted the last heavy obstacle to her freedom. And then running, running, the breathless shouting to Pacifica, who kept falling behind—be quick, don't linger, leave your shoes if they hamper you, we won't be wearing shoes when we are with Francesco. She had not asked herself where she would sleep that night, nor did she care or think she would ever care again, but a few hours later, as she lay sleepless on a straw mattress at the convent of San Paolo, she could only weep bitterly and vow that she would not sleep or eat as long as she was lodged among the Benedictines.

But she had broken that vow, she had been forced to stay; there was nowhere else to go, and when her uncle and his armed men came pounding on the convent door demanding to see her, she was glad enough for the aristocratic hauteur of the old abbess, who expressed in as few words as possible the seriousness of her outrage that the holy peace of her convent should be disturbed on Good Friday, of all days in the year. She subdued these big, rough men though she barely came up to their waists. Still they insisted on seeing Chiara. When they were led to the convent chapel, where the runaway was kneeling, Chiara rushed to the altar, clinging to the cloth with one hand while with the other she pulled back the linen wimple, baring her shorn head. Then they understood. Though she was not a novice, she had sought and received the asylum of the Church. Her uncle berated her, but he could do no more than that, so he went out, followed by his men, without speaking to the abbess, who eyed him with frank hostility and followed him all the way to where the horses stood champing the grass near the convent gate.

Now Chiara makes her hands into fists and throws herself facedown on the cold stones of the chapel floor. She must stand firm, trusting in God and Francesco to save her, for she will not go back to her home; nor will she stay among these women with their dowries and privileges, their carved stalls, their ivory prayer books, the high wooden pattens they wear to keep their pampered feet out of the mud. She will be the noble lady of Francesco's dreams, giving up every comfort, every worldly care, living as he does, a pauper, an outcast. She will follow his way, take his rule as her own, and she will be answerable to no judgment but his.

The heady joy of flight has passed, and Chiara has plummeted back to earth like a wounded dove, struggling all the way. Francesco and her cousin Rufino, Bishop Guido, her father, and her uncle have been up and down the road to the convent a dozen times. Her sister Agnese has run away to join her, so now there are three of them, Chiara, Pacifica, and Agnese, clamoring for their freedom. They want to live as the brothers do, to walk with them into the towns, preaching and begging, or they will live among the lepers and the sick and nurse them. Chiara has wept until her eyes are two red pools in the pallor of her face, and she has refused to eat anything the nuns offer her. When Francesco brings her the bread of the poor which he has begged for her, she consents to take a crumb, but nothing more.

An agreement has been reached. The bishop will donate the church at San Damiano to be used as a convent by the rebellious girls. They will live, as Chiara insists, only on alms; they will have none but the barest furniture and no property save their rough robes. Francesco will write a rule for them, and they will be the Poor Ladies, ever the wards of the Poor Men and of the Church.

They are a solemn party as they file down the mountain path in the sun-drenched spring air, Chiara and Agnese, Pacifica, Bishop Guido, Rufino and Francesco. All around them the earth is bursting with life, and the air is cool and limpid. Fresh green shoots have pushed up through the remains of last year's leaves, and the branches that stretch out to them are tipped with swollen red buds. A nuthatch, creeping headfirst down the trunk of an oak, watches their procession intently. He is silent, though the chatter of his fellows fills the air. Chiara is so weak that she has to clutch her sister's arm to keep from stumbling among the stones. She can see

Francesco at the head of the group, looking back amiably. His wonted pace is quick, but they can't keep up, so he is forced to stop and wait.

It is a long walk down the mountain, past the walls of the town, down again through the olive grove to the poor church. Francesco begged the wooden tiles for the new roof and laid them in with his own hands. The building is shabby but solid and water-tight. The yard before the chapel is hard-packed dirt, and the doors stand open, for the altar is bare. Chiara steps inside to have a look. It is a dark, damp, windowless cave, but the stone floor has been swept clean, and Francesco has strewn an armful of early flowers, heather, wild rose petals, and myrtle, which he gathered in the field nearby, for spring is further advanced here in the valley. She smiles at Francesco as she comes out into the sun, her first smile of the day. Bishop Guido is at the door to the rectory, and he calls out to them the good news that there is some mint in the dooryard and those green shoots are surely onion tops. This area was once a garden and will be again if the lady Chiara should please herself to care for it. She joins him in examining the neglected patch. Near the wall, a rose bush in dire need of pruning has put out new branches in every direction. The bishop joins Francesco and Rufino, who are struggling with the door, which is half off its hinges. When at last they lift it enough to move it, the bottom edge slips over the sill, and the whole thing sags open abruptly, knocking Rufino on his back in the dirt. He gets to his feet, brushing off his robe, while the old door creaks and groans on its single hinge, half in, half out of the frame. They gather around it, peering through the cloud of dust into the dark interior, the future home of the Poor Ladies of Assisi.

The priest who once lived here was as destitute as Francesco, though not by choice. He has left a few sticks of furniture, a bench, a rough hewn table, a burlap mattress stuffed with straw. Chiara runs her hand over the table and leaves a bright streak in the dust. Francesco and Agnese are raising a dust tempest at the window, struggling with the shutter. Chiara shivers; the room is chilly and damp. The wooden bar scrapes against the stone as Francesco slides it free of the sleeve. Agnese shoves hard, the shutter flies open, and a white shaft of sunlight bursts in. Francesco beats his hands against his knees. "You'll need a broom," he says.

The bishop has come no farther than the doorway, where he peers in hopefully, nodding at Chiara. He will gladly supply a broom. Her family is old, powerful, and loyal to the Church. When the Commune drove the nobles out, the Offreduci clan was forced to flee to Perugia, and their fine house in Assisi was sacked by their neighbors. Chiara was still a child when they returned, already a pious, generous creature, but headstrong and impetuous. When her father found her a husband, she refused him and gave her dowry to the poor, so his family withdrew their offer. She refuses to marry anyone, refuses to live at home, refuses the established convents, refuses to eat. Will she refuse this too, the best bargain the bishop could strike for her?

Francesco is leaning backward out the window, gazing up at a swallow's nest he has discovered in the eaves. There are ladies here already, he observes, who will join Chiara and the Poor Ladies in their praise of their Creator. Chiara stands in the middle of the room watching him, a tentative, curious smile playing at the corners of her mouth. Does she imagine that she will see him often thus, leaning in her window in the soft morning light? Does it occur to her, as she looks about nervously at her new home, that she will never leave this place again?

A Sermon

We must be firmly convinced that we have nothing of our own, except our vices and sins.

——ST. FRANCIS OF ASSISI
Rule of 1221

Not one of the Poor Ladies has slept. When the news came as they sat down to dinner last evening, the excitement was so great most failed to eat. Cardinal Ugolino has at last persuaded Father Francesco to come to their convent and provide their starving souls with some words of spiritual sustenance. Their mother Chiara was nearly transported by this news and agreed to take a morsel of bread only because she had promised blessed Francesco she would eat a few grams of food every day, and she did not want him to find any occasion to reproach her on his visit.

As the sisters gather in their plain dark chapel for their morning prayers, though the sun is hours away from rising, they glance nervously at one another, and there are many dark circles beneath their furtive, curious eyes. How long has it been since the holy father last visited this place? Two novices who are nearing their vows have never seen him.

What will be the text of his sermon? How will he choose to strengthen the resolve and refresh the spirit of these women who have and desire nothing in this world but to serve Lady Poverty, providing spiritual comfort and inspiration for their brothers?

In the old days, before Chiara left the world, she often saw Francesco preaching at San Giorgio. His passion so overwhelmed him that his feet moved in little steps, as if dancing to his sermon. She remembers the exaltation she felt when his eye fell upon her and she knew he read in her heart the same burning passion to give up all for the Lord Christ, to be small, poor, plain, abandoned, betrayed, as He was, and as this young man Francesco was, though the world said he had only gone mad.

After matins, Chiara remains on her knees in the bare chapel, pouring out her soul in thanksgiving. Cardinal Ugolino, who visits regularly and never without some provision for the Ladies, a basket of plums or grapes, a pork bone for their soup, or a sack of barley for their porridge, has promised that Francesco will be with him when he comes, and Brother Elia, who confides in Chiara all the doubts of his troubled soul, will come as well. These educated men find solace in the company of the Poor Ladies; the cardinal is wont to say Chiara's conversation is like talking with an angel, and he comes away from his visits aflame with the love of Christ and ashamed of his own sinful life, so full of comforts and ease. But though she never fails to inquire after Francesco, until now he has not come to San Damiano, a place dear to his soul, for it was here that he first understood that God had need of him to repair and purify his church on earth.

As Chiara prays, the sun comes up. She leaves the chapel and walks out to the garden, where the geraniums spill over the walls studded with velvety blossoms, and the roses perfume the air. She stops to break off a sprig of rosemary, recalling Francesco's recommendation that the sisters grow flowers as well as herbs, because flowers so gladden the heart and remind all men to praise God as they do, with joyful abandon and without concern for the future. This garden will delight his eye, as will the scrubbed floor of the chapel, the plain bare cross in the refectory where the Ladies share their poor meals. She has so much to show him, to tell him, about the progress of their order and about the interior of her own well-scoured soul. She raises her face to the sun, and as she does, she sees at the top of the hill three figures making their way toward the convent, two garbed in gray flanking one robed in black, with a wide-brimmed hat shielding his face from the sun. He is coming. He is coming to his little plant. Impulsively, she pushes back the folds of her wimple and raises her hand to wave.

His mood is somber. He greets the sisters kindly, but does not appear to distinguish one from the other. They are avid; Chiara has to quiet one of the novices with a frown. The cardinal is effusive, as always, delighted to be in the company of his protégé, this brilliant star in the firmament of God's saints on earth. Brother Elia watches Francesco closely, as if studying how to imitate him, though not like poor simple Brother Giovanni, who thought to find salvation by miming Francesco's every move, but intently, patiently, as one might try to decipher a difficult text. Francesco does not smile until they enter the chapel. He steps inside ahead of the others, leans against the wall, the stones of which he laid himself, and when he turns back to Chiara, she sees that he is happy. He bends upon her a look of such affection and tenderness that her heart expands in the warmth of it. "How beautifully you have kept it all," he says.

But the moment is fleeting. The cardinal, speaking to Elia, presses in behind her, and Francesco enters their conversation. Then the sisters file in, taking their places around the room, arranging the skirts of their robes as they kneel upon the dirt floor. Francesco whispers something to Elia, who goes to Chiara. "He wants a bucket of ashes," Elia says. Chiara nods, calls one of the novices, and dispatches her to the hearth in the refectory. Francesco has wandered toward the altar, which Chiara has strewn with wild thyme and rose petals. He takes up a sprig of thyme, inhaling its fragrance as he turns to his audience, this eager gathering of women. Most of them are from good families. Chiara's clan, the powerful, haughty Offreduci, are well represented: her sisters, cousins, even her mother is there near the door, kneeling on the ground, her hands folded modestly across her waist.

The novice returns with the ashes, which Chiara carries to Francesco. She is so curious and excited that her hand trembles as she sets the bucket down before him, the holy father, the protector of the Poor Ladies. As she backs away, she looks up into his face, but he is staring into the bucket, his lips pressed together in a grim line. He reaches down, plunges one hand deep into the ashes, and brings up a handful. He takes a few steps toward the fascinated sisters and begins sprinkling the ashes at his feet. Then he returns to the bucket and repeats the process. The Poor Ladies are silent; they hardly dare breathe, so deep is their mystification. Chiara takes the opportunity to examine Francesco closely, to see if he has changed. His skin is tanned by the sun. He is thinner, but he does not look unwell. The robe he is wearing is held together by patches; one sleeve is several inches shorter than the other, doubtless torn off to mend other parts. He has an aura of enormous energy under strict control, and he is entirely absorbed in this strange ritual. Soon Francesco and the bucket are closed inside a ring of ash. He holds a handful of ash out before him. Slowly, he raises his hand, and as the sisters draw in a communal breath, he drops the ashes over his head, spreading them with his palm across his forehead and in a circle around his tonsure. Some bits settle on his nose and cheeks. His eyes are closed. He opens his hands before him as if to draw his audience into his embrace. His voice rings out, filling the soundless room—"Have mercy upon me, O God, according to thy lovingkindness: according unto the multitude of thy tender mercies blot out my transgressions."

Is this his text? But how could it be? This is the psalm of David, after he went in to Bathsheba. Chiara glances at Brother Elia, who keeps his head bowed, but the corner of his mouth flickers. Is it amusement or disdain? Francesco's voice drones on. He speaks in a monotone, though now and then he applies a stress or pauses momentarily, as if trying to remember the next word. "Hide thy face from my sins, and blot out all my iniquities."

This is his message to them, in their poverty, their humility, their obedience, their chastity, their suffering, in the endless cycle of their days far from the world's eye.

"Cast me not away from thy presence; and take not thy holy spirit from me."

Chiara cannot bring herself even to look at him. He has come to remind them of how sinful they are, and of the ash they will become.

"Deliver me from bloodguiltiness, O God, thou God of my salvation."

His voice grows stronger, more confident, as he nears the end. He drops soundlessly to his knees, his hands pressed together. "The sacrifices of God are a broken spirit; a broken and a contrite heart, O God, thou wilt not despise."

For some time, Chiara realizes, there has been another sound besides his voice. All around her, the Poor Ladies cover their eyes with their hands, and the tears flow down their faces. One mutters, "Christ have mercy"; another cries out, "Deliver me, O God of my salvation." Francesco gets to his feet and looks out over the group, then steps into their midst, moving quickly toward the back of the chapel.

Chiara does not watch him go. His long-awaited visit is over, she knows this, and he has said what he thinks the Poor Ladies need to hear. Tears fill her eyes too, but she does not call on God to save her. Elia rises and follows Francesco out the door. The cardinal, off to her right, does not move. He will doubtless stay to dinner, having brought with him a chicken from his own yard to add to the humble board of the Poor Ladies.

A Last Visit to the Poor Ladies

*The belief in the punishing or rewarding omnipotence of God,
never has in itself a "civilizing" or affect-subduing effect.
On the contrary, religion is always exactly as "civilized"
as the society or class which upholds it.*

—NORBERT ELIAS
The Civilizing Process: The History of Manners

In her illness Chiara fears she might die without seeing him again, and she dreads this possibility more than she fears the fires of hell, so she sends a messenger begging him to come to her as soon as possible. The messenger returns with a note from Brother Elia saying Francesco has bid him give her his promise, that before she dies she will see him again. She is scarcely consoled, for Elia concludes with the news that Francesco is so near death he is not expected to live out the week. She swoons and lies upon her bed in a stupor for three days, then she opens her eyes and is well. All around her the Poor Ladies sleep peacefully. She leaves her cot, climbs up to her rooftop garden, and looks west, toward the Portiuncula where they have taken him from the bishop's house.

It is a clear, cool, starry night. Over the hills the sky glows red from the torches, and she can hear the distant sound of voices; the whole town is there. Alone on her rooftop, Chiara understands that Francesco has died. She prays for him and to him, softly, her eyes dry, her heart curiously calm. She does not doubt that he will keep his promise.

Toward morning the sisters wake up, dress, and gather in the chapel for matins. Chiara tells them nothing, keeping the secret close to her heart. As they come out into the portico, they see a stranger on horseback, riding at a gallop down the hill toward the convent. Chiara hurries the sisters inside and stays in the foyer, serving as porter herself. The visitor does not knock but throws open the door to find Chiara sitting composedly on the stone bench. He is a boy, sweating and panting, his eyes red from weeping with the others. He has come, he announces, with a message from Brother Elia to be delivered to Mother Chiara and no other.

Chiara nods. "I am Mother Chiara," she says. She hears a whisper from behind the door to the refectory and the sound of shuffling feet. This message will be delivered to the community at large.

The boy gathers his wits, standing up straight and puffing out his chest. Brother Elia has sent him, he explains, with news at once woeful and joyful. This night the Lord Christ has taken Blessed Brother Francesco to sit with him in the firmament of heaven, with all the other saints, leaving us bereft, like lost sheep whose shepherd has been called away.

A stifled sob issues from the next room. The boy stops, studies the door, then looks at Chiara, who has not moved and keeps her eyes fastened to his face. Brother Elia also says, he continues, that the friars will carry the earthly remains of Blessed Francesco to San Giorgio to be buried this morning, and that their route will pass the convent of the Poor Ladies so they may bid farewell to their beloved brother and father Francesco.

Chiara nods again, but she does not speak. The boy stands pulling at his shirt, which is too small for him and ragged at the sleeves. They both listen to the voices behind the door. The sisters no longer make any pretense at not being there. They hear soft cries addressed to God, sobs of dismay. Chiara touches her fingers to her face as if she feels uncertain that her head is still there. "Thank you," she says, without looking up. "You may go."

She allows them all to go up on the roof so that they may see the procession as it makes the long descent to their convent door. The weeping is contagious, it moves from one sister to another; Chiara herself is not immune. The sun is high in the sky when they hear the sound of trumpets. They see a few boys running ahead, then the clutch of trumpeters in their bright coats, then the branches of what looks like a moving forest. This forest is singing hymns of praise, the sisters know them well, and the singers wave their branches in time with the music. Though it is day, there are torchbearers flanking the group, keeping the flames well away from the branches. Behind the citizens, preceded by a band of torches like a sheet of flame, come the friars. Their heads are bowed, they stride purposefully in a close rank, adding their voices to the chorus. Chiara leans against the wall of the roof terrace, trying to distinguish one brother from the next. At the front is Elia, she recognizes his squarish blue-black beard, and there is Leone, whose beard is flowing and white. Her cousin Angelo— she knows him by his knightly bearing—walks sedately near the back. Then, cresting the hill, Chiara sees what she has prayed she would never see, aloft on the shoulders of eight friars, moving swiftly toward her as if on a current of air, the plain wooden coffin in which they have laid him. Around this coffin there is a great press of humanity, prelates carrying gold and silver crosiers, wealthy men in heavy robes embroidered with jewels, women in simple wool garments with dark veils covering their faces, ragged children, shepherds with their staffs, even a few pilgrims in their short scalloped coats, who have, unexpectedly, found another saint to add to the list of those visited on their pilgrimage.

The trumpets have arrived at the doors of the convent, and they give such a blast that the Poor Ladies cover their ears. They press close to their mother, weeping and complaining. What are they to do? How are they to see the holy father? They cannot go out in such a crowd as this. Chiara urges them down the steps and into the refectory, where they must wait until she has consulted with Brother Elia. She leaves them there, hurries along the passage to the chapel, and pulls back the bar at the low door. Then she waits in the shadows, listening to the voices and the mill of activity outside the door. Something brushes her ankle; she starts, stifling a shout. It is the convent cat who has followed her, hoping to go outside in the sun. For several moments the nun and the cat wait together quietly. Then the door opens, the cat rushes out, and Brother Elia steps in. "God grant you peace, dear lady," he says, taking Chiara's hands in his own. She draws herself away and does not look at him.

"He died quietly," he says. "He was trying to sing."

"What was he singing?" she asks.

"Educ de custodia animam meam."

She smiles but makes no comment. Elia looks about the chapel. Outside, the singers have begun a new hymn, calling on God to send St. Michael to carry blessed Francesco's soul into eternal light.

"We will bring him in here," Elia says. "Open the communion window and the sisters will see him there."

"I will go and prepare them," she replies. As she steps back into the passage, he touches her arm. "He is much altered," he says. Chiara hurries away.

By the time the Poor Ladies have gathered at the window, the friars have brought the coffin into the chapel and bolted the door behind them. Chiara goes first and looks into the chapel to see them pulling the lid off the coffin. Elia leans over one side, blocking her view, but she can see the lower part of Francesco's robe and his feet. The wounds are like two brown leaves lying against the white flesh, as if they fell there when they passed under the trees on the road. Two friars she does not recognize kneel on the far side of the coffin. At a word from Elia, they slip their arms beneath the corpse and lift it out of the box. A sister among those pressed near her moans, "Father, Father, what shall we do?" Elia steps aside and the two friars approach the window, cradling the corpse like a sleeping child in their arms.

How pale he is, how white this flesh that was once so swarthy. Even his reddish beard is faded to gold. His mouth is slightly open and his teeth show white as milk, and at the edge of his eyelids there is a thin line of nacreous white, as if his eyes were made of pearl. Chiara says only his name: "Francesco." Is it truly him? The Poor Ladies now crowd one another, weeping and crying out, taking brief turns at the window, then turning away to wail. "Who will comfort us in our poverty?" one cries, and another, "Oh most bitter separation, oh most dreadful death that slays the sons and daughters bereft of so great a father." The friars bring the body closer, holding him up so that the Poor Ladies can reach out and touch him. One of the novices strokes his neck and shoulder, convulsed in tears. "What do you bid us do, Father," she murmurs, "shut up in this prison?"

Elia approaches, positioning himself alongside the window. He whispers to Chiara, "See how beautiful he is." Tears burst from her eyes, flooding up from her chest as if to wring the blood from her heart. It is him, he is there, and he is gone. She will never hear his voice again. She can see him, dancing before her on the moonlit trail that night, nearly fifteen years ago, when she ran from her father's house to his protection. And before that, she can see him when she was returning from the market and the boys were chasing him through the street, pelting him with mud and calling him madman, clown, fool; she can see his weary smile as, dodging their fury, he missed his step and fell full-length in the mud at her feet.

"Why do you forsake us?" one of the Poor Ladies begs, pressing her back to the wall and sliding down into a pool of misery. Elia lifts the dead arm, raising the hand close to the window. "See how flexible he is," he says, his voice full of wonder. Chiara reaches out to touch this hand, to take it in her own, as she takes the host from the priest at this window. Gently she turns the palm up and raises it to her face, gently she kisses the wound, closing her eyes as the cold fingertips press against her brow and she tastes the dried blood liquefying in her tears.

On His Youth and Conversion

In Hiding, in Chains

The men of that time had all the vices except triviality, all the virtues except moderation; they were either ruffians or saints. Life was rude enough to kill feeble organisms; and thus characters had an energy unknown today.

—PAUL SABATIER
St. Francis of Assisi

He can hear their voices, angry and exultant over the terrified cries of their prisoners, like the shouts of butchers one to another when they are herding the squealing, struggling pigs into the slaughtering pen. These captors are neither men nor beasts; in spite of their hairy backs, black horns, brutish snouts, and birdlike feet, they stand upright and brandish in their large human hands the tools of their trade, lashes, slashing-hooks, glowing, red-hot irons. One digs his talons into the neck of a naked man who writhes beneath him, his face swollen and blue, his body drawn up in an impossible arc. His mouth is opened wide in a howl, for his captor has forced a thick rod between his buttocks and is bearing down hard upon it. Behind these two, a woman has fallen to her knees as she struggles to release her shoulder from the jaws of another demon. The creature's thick, reptilian tail is wrapped around her torso, holding her fast against his thighs. He mocks her suffering, pointing out her destination: a black tube with teeth, like the mouth of an enormous serpent, down which two of his fellows have deposited another victim, whether male or female is uncertain, because only the legs and feet are visible. The feet are curiously flexed. The prisoners are all naked but for two—a man in rich garb, carrying a sack across his shoulders and entering the awful scene through a flaming gate at one side, and another man crawling on the ground near the serpent mouth, his torso wrapped tightly in the coiled tail of another demon, naked but for his bishop's miter, still firmly in place on his head. The bishop gazes at another man, who has a demon crouched upon his stomach. The creature is positioned so that his buttocks are poised just over his victim's face; his sharp talons are sunk in the man's genitals. The sufferer's mouth is held

open by an iron device, his eyes are rolled back in agony and horror. From the demon's anus flows an endless stream of gold coins,
filling the open mouth, choking the man with gold.

Francesco lets out a soft huff of amusement as he examines this
last image. He looks up from the dark and lurid sufferings of the
damned to the bright sunlit window next to him, but he does not
notice the limpidity of the light which illuminates the book and
table he is bending over, for he hears the sound of footsteps on the
gravel outside. Hurriedly, he crosses the room and drops down into
an open recess in the floor, a space so narrow and shallow he has to
curl himself in a ball to fit into it. He reaches up to slide the flat
stone that serves as a lid for this, his own personal hell, into place,
closing his eyes tight against the shower of dirt that always drifts
down when the edge lodges into the earth. Within a few moments,
he has breathed up all the available oxygen, and he feels the con-
striction in his chest, like a ribbon of steel tightening around his
heart. He keeps one hand cupped over his nose, because this gives
him the illusion that he is filtering out the dirt and allowing in
something remotely breathable. Then, for what seems a long time,
he is still, listening, waiting, all his senses absorbed in determining
the nature of the activity above the floor. The door has opened,
the intruder has paused, then the footsteps come purposefully
to the hiding place. Two sharp raps bring down a fresh shower of
dirt. At once he pushes up with all his strength, lifting the stone
until his friend is able to grasp the edge and pull it back across the
floor. Francesco sits up in his hole and rubs the dirt from his eyes.

"Your father has not relented," the old priest says breathlessly.
He has come from the town as fast as he can walk, bringing a loaf
of barley bread, a flask of quince wine, and the latest installment in
the never-ending chronicle of bad news for Francesco. "He knows
you are in hiding hereabouts," he continues, "and he has sworn to
find you if he has to pay the entire guard."

Francesco gets to his feet and takes his friend's hand as he steps
out of his prison. "He won't have to pay anyone," he says flatly.

The priest throws up his hands in a gesture of dismay. "What will you do?"

"I'm going to Assisi," Francesco says. "He will find me in the street easily enough."

He is barely inside the gate when the trouble begins. Two boys returning from the forest, each burdened by a large dead hare, push past him, and he is so weak that he staggers into the wall. Their heads come up, their eyes fix coldly upon him, and their nostrils quiver, testing the air, deciphering the scent of vulnerability and fear. "Idiot," one observes. Francesco rights himself and continues up the street, holding the skirt of his tunic around his knees so that he will not trip upon it. The boys fall into step behind him. They are each half his size, each has twice his strength. "You know who this is," one says to the other. "This is the son of Pietro Bernardone, the one who has robbed his father and disgraced his name." Francesco plods on, keeping his eyes on the stones rising ahead of him. He can feel the muscles in his calves tightening, unused to even this undemanding exercise.

"Why have you come back, madman?" one of the boys taunts him. "Do you think your father will welcome you?" The other steps up quickly, overtaking Francesco and darting out ahead of him, dangling his hare by its ears. He squeezes his nose with his free hand and whines, "God, how he stinks."

"He stinks of his friends at the *lazaretto*," his companion offers. "He is searching for his new love among the lepers." At this remark, Francesco looks briefly over his shoulder, his expression a complex of exhaustion, fever, and irony. The boy feels the hot black arrow of this regard as a momentary hesitation, banished before he notices it by the arrival of a trio clattering down the stone steps from San Giorgio. They are just released from school and wild from a morning of Latin declensions, intent now on merriment or mischief, whichever comes easiest. At once they spy

Francesco and his two persecutors and rush forward to join in the game, shouting imprecations—idiot, swine, thief, madman. Circling Francesco, they pluck at his sleeves, bump him hard with their hips and elbows, mocking his efforts to keep his footing and continue on his way. His resistance is feeble, and he does not protest, which excites their contempt so that they speak for him, grinning and winking at one another: "Oh, do not push me so, my dear Giorgio"; "Matteo, why are you so rough with me?" The racket brings women to the upper windows along the street. A few are so curious they open their doors and step out to see what the excitement is about. "It is Pietro Bernardone's son," one informs the other. Like a feather riding upon the air, this phrase is borne along the streets, fluttering across the piazza at San Giorgio, sucked into the narrow passageway and puffed out across the marketplace where the stalls are closing for the day and the old women trudging homeward with their baskets half empty—for summer is over, and already there is little to buy but turnips, apples, and quince—lift their sharp faces to hear the news: "Pietro's son Francesco has come back."

Francesco is right; his father finds him easily enough. As he makes his way through the town, his mocking entourage thickens so that he can scarcely see what is ahead. The children pick up stones and clods of dirt, which they pitch at him, shouting with delight if they hit their mark. Francesco plods on, indifferent, but when they pass the ancient columns of Minerva's temple, the press in front of him suddenly parts, and he is faced with a sight that weakens his legs, though not his resolve. His father rushes toward him, bellowing, cursing, calling on God and on all his neighbors to witness his disgrace and his fury. His face is bright red, his eyes bulge in their sockets, his lips are pulled back over his teeth like an enraged dog's. Francesco stands his ground, but at the last, as his father charges down upon him, he throws up his hands to protect his face.

"Ingrate," Pietro shouts, grabbing his son by the hair. "Thief, scoundrel!" He knocks Francesco to his knees with a backhanded blow, then jerks him up and slaps him across the ear.

Francesco does not struggle or cry out. He has been living in a hole for a month, refining his courage for this confrontation, and though the father has superior strength, the son's will has been formed, like igneous rock, under pressure, and it is as unyielding as granite.

The crowd, fickle and intemperate, now takes the side of youth against age and chides Pietro for his anger. This criticism stings, and he protests vociferously. How could they know what he has been through for twenty-four years, day after day, with this good-for-nothing boy who claims he has God's blessing to steal from his own father? He grips Francesco by the elbow and pulls him forward so roughly he feels the sinew pop at the shoulder, but he will not be stopped now. If the boy resists, he will take his arm right out of the socket. Francesco reels, his eyes roll back in his head, and he stumbles forward, endeavoring to keep up. Pietro rains down curses on his son, his neighbors, his town, the world, on God himself, who has cursed him with the infamy of an ungrateful son. The crowd parts; no one wants to be in the path of his rage. As he drags Francesco toward the house where his mother stands crying in the doorway, his neighbors lean out of their windows, shouting, "Shame! Shame upon such a father who drives his son away" and "Shame upon his house and his whole family."

"Out of my way," Pietro shouts to his wife, who backs into the house until she runs into a chest and sits down upon it. She presses her hands to either side of her wimple to close out the sound of her husband's curses. Francesco casts her a look as he is dragged from the room, but not, as she might wish, a helpless, pleading look, which she could meet with tears and pleading of her own. No, his jaw is set, his eyes are full of defiance, it is a look to match his father's, and seeing that the resolution of this quarrel will not come with ease, she opens her mouth and wails after her husband and her son, "Francesco, Pietro. For the love of God."

"Enough," Pietro shouts back to her as he hauls his son into the second room and yanks open the door to the cellar. "I have had enough." Down the few steps he drags his son, holding him by the hair so that he cannot stand, and when they are inside the damp, chilly room, he gives him a sideways kick that knocks him to the floor. "Where is my money?" he shouts. Francesco rolls to his knees and makes for the door, but Pietro catches him by the foot and drags him back, howling his complaint now—"Where is my money? Where is my horse?"

It is not to be borne. It cannot be borne. He will disown his son, he will have him banned from the town. If he wants to beg, then let him go beg where no one knows him and no one cares whether he lives or not, far from his father's offended eyes. He will give everything to Angelo, who is a dutiful son; Angelo shall have it all. As he rages, Pietro drags Francesco across the floor to a chest in which grain is stored, and begins loosening the chain that attaches it to an iron ring in the wall. He will lock up this wayward son, just as he locks up his grain and his bolts of fine linen, wool, and silk, and his house and all his furniture and everything that is his. If God wants to come and speak to Francesco, let him do it in his father's house, and let God explain to him, to Pietro Bernardone, why any man should be cursed with such a son.

A father. A son. Pietro cannot stop laboring the connection, and Francesco does not deny it. He has become quiet, pliant; he keeps his eyes down as his father fastens one loop of chain around his ankle and another around his neck, so that he is forced to sit with his back against the wall and one knee drawn up to his chest. A final clout to the head, a final remonstration—How can you humiliate me? I have given you everything! I gave you your life!—and the father strides away. In the open doorway, Francesco's mother stands trembling, wringing her hands. The sight of her is like a poker thrust into a bed of embers, churning up a last burst of flame. "Get away from him," Pietro cries. "He will stay there until he gives me back what he has stolen." He slams the door behind him so forcefully it rebounds in the frame, and he has to close it a second time.

Francesco sits motionless as the blackness floods in like water. He can hear his mother wailing, his father's steady cursing. Francesco will stay there, Pietro replies to his wife's tearful entreaty, and he will have nothing to eat but bread and water. And that is how it will be for as long as he says it will be, for as long as it takes to bring that madman to his senses.

Francesco presses his head against the wall and shifts his body toward it. This position creates enough slack in the chain to let him stretch his leg almost all the way out.

A Lesson from the Gospels

Man has as much knowledge as he puts to work.

—ST. FRANCIS OF ASSISI
The Mirror of Perfection

Francesco dresses as a hermit, but it is another of his fantasies, for he continually appears in the town. It is just as it was when he decided to become a knight and a crusader: his father spent a fortune on his wardrobe, equipped him with a proper horse, lance, armor, even hired a steward, and off he went to join Walter of Brienne, but he got no farther than Spoleto before he gave up the idea and came home. He offered no explanation for his decision, so his father could only shrug when people asked what had become of his son's grand ambition. It is a scandal to see this father curse his son when they chance to meet on some street corner, but surely a father has rarely been so hard pressed by a son as Pietro Bernardone has been by his oldest boy. Francesco has stolen from Pietro, repudiated him in public, and disowned himself, denying his father even that bitter pleasure. Now the mad son goes about in rags, leaning on a staff like an Old Testament prophet and begging his former neighbors for bread, and for stones and oil as well, for he is not idle. He has finished the repairs at San Damiano and moved on to the poor ruin of the Church of the Blessed Virgin in the woods of the Portiuncula, where the monks on Mount Subasio allow him to stay, for it is their chapel he is repairing. They send a priest down to say mass for him, and that is all the company he has there.

The priest counsels the young man as best he can, but finds him a difficult case, vacillating between shame over his former sinful life, sorrow at the thought of Christ's suffering for those sins, and a wild optimism about the course by which he will reconcile his past sins with his present virtue. God, he says, has told him to rebuild poor, abandoned churches like this one, where he works and lives, solitary, friendless, but full of hope. Naturally, his progress is slow, but he never seems to despair or lose patience when he is working. And those who have seen his work agree: for a rich man's son, Francesco is an excellent stonemason.

All the way down the road from Mount Subasio, the priest has sunk to his knees in the snow; but once he reaches the wood near the Portiuncula, the going is easier, for he can walk in the path Francesco has worn carrying his stones down from the town. In the clearing, he finds his charge sitting in the doorway of the roofless chapel, waiting patiently, his pale shanks exposed to the cold which he never seems to notice. There is no sign of a fire. He has slept among his stones and tools, his hair is still wet from the snow. He greets the Benedictine cheerfully, as he always does, with the words "God grant you peace, Father Angelo," and follows him through the doorway to the inside of the chapel, which is very like the outside. The floor is strewn with stones, and the sun streams through the open roof, melting the snow into a network of rivulets that run off in every direction. The two men talk idly for a few minutes. Sometimes a woodcutter who works in the forest joins them, or the old priest from San Damiano, who is devoted to Francesco, comes for the mass, always bringing a little bread or a turnip he has saved for his favorite. The ancient altar stone is still there, smooth and flat, and the priest lays out his cloth, his pyx, his flask of holy wine. Francesco watches, fascinated by every detail. He responds to the opening antiphon of the mass in a clear, high voice with the careful intonation of a student having his Latin examined. Father Angelo finds his manner naive but not without charm; a pleasant change from the droning of the monks in the abbey, or the confused mumbling of the goatherds and shepherds who attend the chapel on the grounds. When he reads out the lessons, Francesco stands, his hands clasped, his back straight, and his eyes narrowed, as if he thought he could improve his hearing by squinting. During the Gospel the priest notices his communicant's lips moving silently over the words he recognizes. *"Euntes autem praedicate," "nolite possidere,"* and *"non peram in via."* When the priest places the host on his tongue, Francesco's eyes close, and he sways backward as if he is being pushed, so that he must take a small step to keep his balance.

Father Angelo knows Bishop Guido has tried repeatedly to persuade the young man to join the Benedictines, but Francesco refuses, determined to go on with his maniacal building. Perhaps he only wants to reproach his father, who could forget this son if he was behind the abbey walls and turn his attention to his second boy, also named Angelo, already a shrewd businessman, able to cheat his neighbors and drive a bargain as interminably as any Jew. When the townspeople mock Francesco on the street, his brother joins in. People say their mother hasn't stopped weeping for two years.

The mass has ended. Father Angelo cleans out his horn cup with snow and dries it on his own sleeve. Usually Francesco is elated by receiving the sacraments, but today he seems distracted and agitated. He asks the priest if he would be willing to stay a little longer, would he go over some lines in the Gospel, for his own Latin is very poor, he is an idiot, and he does not wish to make a mistake about something so important. The priest agrees; he is not in a hurry. They will sit in the sun on one of Francesco's stones and read the lesson together.

They choose a seat near the doorway, and Francesco brushes off the surface with a flourish, as if preparing a place for the pope. The swallows fly in one window and out the door, then loop back over the open roof, their chittering cry like a shiver. The two men sit side by side, and Father Angelo opens his bible to the ribbon he has used to mark the day's reading. Though Francesco is still, the priest can feel his excitement, which seems out of keeping with the situation. There is something edgy and panicked about him, like a deer poised for flight. He bends his head over the page and puts out his hand tentatively. He touches the blue and gold letter at the beginning of the passage, then withdraws his finger quickly as if embarrassed by his own impetuosity. Father Angelo notices the appalling condition of the hand, which is red and chapped, the knuckles swollen and bruised, deep unhealed scrapes across three of them. The nails are jagged, the thumbnail torn to the quick. The wrist, too, is swollen and bruised black from the base of the thumb to the edge of the sleeve. It is more eloquent, more touching, than a laborer's hand, for there is none of the muscle and sinew that come with a lifetime of toil; this hand is small, refined, the fingers taper gracefully, the wrist bones stand out under the flesh like knobs of white marble. The sight of this delicate, abused hand startles the priest. Like a torchlight flaring up in a black night, the impression of it, of the moment of actually seeing it, sputters behind his eyes, and he blinks involuntarily.

He remembers seeing Francesco in the piazza of San Giorgio one summer evening a few years ago in the company, as he always was, of a rowdy group of friends. He had organized them into a singing group, "the Company of Tripudiates," and they went about singing the latest songs from Provence or putting on impromptu pageants, playing out the old stories of Charlemagne, Arthur, and Merlin. They were high-spirited, well-dressed, convivial, empty-headed young men, outdoing one another in foolishness, the darlings of doting mothers who smiled and shouted down greetings and warnings from the windows to their sons cavorting in the streets below. That evening the priest had paused to look at Francesco, who was seated on a low stone wall, his many-colored cloak thrown back over his shoulders to show the rich green silk surcoat underneath. He was leaning back on one hand and encouraging one of his clownish comrades by making a circular motion with the other, his mouth slightly ajar, his dark eyes full of delight, his shoulders bent forward over his narrow chest, shaking with laughter. Everyone but his father knew at a glance that this youth was not a future cloth merchant. The friction between father and son was already the subject of gossip from one end of the town to another. Father Angelo, eyeing the foppish, useless young man on the wall, had thought—What will become of him?

Now he knew that his wildest imaginings had failed to conjure up anything as unexpected and mysterious as what had actually become of Francesco. If he had said to himself—He will be transformed—would he, even then, have been close? Could anyone, seeing the carefree, passionate, vain young peacock Francesco was then, have looked into his future and predicted the difficult and solitary path he would choose?

Francesco clears his throat and reads out the first words of the lesson haltingly in his schoolboy Latin: "*Et convocatis duodecim discipulis suis.* And he called his twelve disciples." The priest nods. Francesco is not, as he called himself, an idiot. Though he reads slowly, he has a good understanding and translates with almost pedantic precision. The priest corrects him, but not often. When he does, Francesco is patient; he listens to the explanation of a grammatical point, his eyes darting back and forth from the printed words to Father Angelo's face. When they reach the line in which Christ tells the disciples to take no shoes as they go out to preach, Francesco pauses and looks down at his own shabby footwear, castoffs from the priest at San Damiano. Father Angelo follows his student's gaze indulgently. There are cracks along the seams, a gaping hole over one toe, and he has fastened the loose tops around his ankles with thin strips of leather. The priest does not think God would begrudge any man such shoes as these.

Francesco returns to the text, rendering the passage in his careful translation. "Take no gold for your journey, nor silver, nor copper in your belts, no purse for your journey, nor two tunics, nor sandals, nor a staff . . ." His voice trails off at the last words, and he lifts his head.

"That's correct," the priest says.

Francesco looks off into the maze of bare trees and snow that was once and will be again a luxuriant forest. He presses his lips together, lost in thought. An eerie stillness descends. Again the priest follows Francesco's gaze, looking out at the forest as if he could find there the subject of his student's reverie. But he sees nothing, only a chilly winter scene, bathed in light but without warmth, and so quiet he can hear the slow drip of the snow melting on a branch at the clearing's edge. Francesco raises his hand to his chin, smoothing his beard between his thumb and fingers, but still his thoughts are turned inward and he does not speak. An icy breeze wraps itself around Father Angelo's ankles, then lifts the parchment of the book lying open in his lap. Francesco returns his attention to the book.

"Nor two tunics," he repeats, "nor sandals, nor a staff."

"That's correct," the priest says.

Francesco nods his head slowly. "This is it," he says softly.

The priest moves his finger down the page, for they have, in his opinion, sufficiently treated these lines, but Francesco does not follow his lead. He turns to his teacher, takes him by the arm, and in a voice trembling with emotion says, "This is what I wish. This is what I seek." He releases the priest and bends over his ankles, pulling at the knotted straps of his shoe. Father Angelo looks down at him, his forehead creased with dismay. The laces give way. Francesco pulls off the shoe and tosses it to one side, then sets himself to untying the other. "This is what I long to do with all my heart," he exclaims. Father Angelo snaps the book closed in his lap. The lessons are over.

A Penitent; in the Background, a Hermit

Pilgrimages were not only a common form of religious penance: they were frequently imposed as civil penalties as well. With a safe-conduct valid only along a certain prescribed pilgrimage route, an undesirable was out of the way but never beyond surveillance.

—CAROLLY ERICKSON
The Medieval Vision

May God have mercy on the penitent Roberto. In the morning he is at the city gates, standing apart from the crowd, his head bowed over his staff. The others are the usual: merchants, beggars, a swineherd, a stonemason and his apprentice, a messenger from Spoleto, a Basque with his inevitable dried fish to sell, a poor knight of Le Marche, two nervous, garrulous women, both slaves who have lingered outside the walls after dark and spent the night dreading the beating they will soon receive in their master's house, an old priest on his way to Terni, where he has been called by his bishop, and the woodcutter who lives near Mount Subasio and has come down with his ass and cart to deliver a load of wood to the baker. In response to the taunting of his fellow travelers, the penitent has produced a letter from the Lord Pope Innocent himself, which is passed from hand to hand among those who can read it, and all who do recoil, for it describes both the heinous and unnatural crime this man has committed and the harsh sentence the pope has prescribed for its expiation. The knight returns the parchment to Roberto with tears in his eyes, for he once spent six months in a Saracen prison and, he confides, not one day passed when he did not thank God his wife and child were not with him. One of the merchants takes a small loaf from his horse's pack and brings it to the man. The old priest approaches with him, but to the surprise of everyone present, he curses this Roberto and spits upon him, then strides purposefully away.

The penitent accepts everything—horror, sympathy, bread, abuse—with the same humble, exhausted gratitude. He doesn't bother even to wipe the sputum from his beard. His hair is thick and matted; it comes down low on his forehead like a felted cap.

His eyes are dark, ringed in flesh the color of a bruise, his hands are cracked and the nails black. He folds his letter and slips it inside his tunic, and the knight, who has been calculating the days, observes that he must be nearly at the end of his penance.

The look Roberto gives him is mocking; does the knight imagine there can be an end to the working out of such a crime? But he speaks politely, in accents that suggest both education and breeding. He is on his way to Roma, it is true. He has been as far west as Compostela and as far north as Canterbury, and for three years has never rested two nights in the same place. He has stopped here to visit the shrine of San Rufino, to present his letter to the priest, and to receive his discipline as the letter commands. The knight listens thoughtfully, looking past the ragged man to the crowd gathering at the gates, for the hour has come—the gatekeepers have raised the bar, and the iron hinges groan in protest, yielding, as they do each morning, to the urgent press of business upon the still sleeping town of Assisi.

The knight and the penitent hang back, then go in together, for the knight has offered himself as a guide to the church, which he knows well. News of the penitent and his letter runs ahead of them: it excites the imagination and loosens the tongues of all who hear it. Only the old priest is not waylaid by the pleasure of gossip. As the citizens yank open their doors, and shouting children, chickens, barking dogs, and half-dressed servants emerge into the bright daylight, he rushes by, undistracted, though he is careful to dodge the rain of night waste from the upper windows. He turns into a narrow alley to find two pigs blocking the way. Calling on God to protect him, he plunges ahead, pushing against their heavy sides, but instead of moving on, they panic, squealing and kicking his shins with their hooves. He pounds on their backs, which so enrages the beasts that they attack him in earnest, tearing off bits of his robe. One manages to sink his sharp teeth through the cloth and into his new enemy's thigh.

So it is that the priest arrives at the doors of San Rufino some minutes later, limping pitifully, his robe in shreds, blood running down his leg into his shoe. But he ignores his own suffering, so eager is he to inform the vicar (whom he knows well; they were students together in Bologna) of the important obligation coming his way. He bursts into the vestibule, raising his arms and calling out excitedly, "Father Bernabo, come at once. They will be here soon."

And he is correct. The knight and the penitent have reached the ancient temple of Minerva at the head of a procession of children, dogs, women, old men, and even a few tradesmen, who have turned their stalls over to their disgruntled assistants, for everyone wants to witness the spectacle. The penitent goes slowly, muttering his prayers and pausing every few steps to bend his knee, which makes his attendants impatient. They push and shout at one another while the knight chastises them, knocking those who try to molest the penitent back into the crowd. These prayers, he protests, are part of the penance they have come to witness, and anyone who obstructs them goes against God's will as well as the Lord Pope's express decree, imperiling thereby his or her own immortal soul. They round the last corner, and the penitent stops to look across the piazza at the facade of San Rufino. The doors stand open. Between the two stone lions that guard the holy relics within, the two priests wait for him side by side, their arms folded severely. Father Bernabo is holding a short rod from the end of which depend several thin strips of leather. When he sees the crowd, he unfolds his arms and passes the rod from one hand to the other awkwardly, as if he has been caught with some damning evidence.

Francesco has left his work at the chapel to walk up to the town and beg for food. The old priest would surely offer him some of his own meager provisions, but Francesco does not like to take advantage of this charity, which has been so ready and so constant.

The sun is up; it is already hot, the air abuzz with insects. He walks briskly through the olive grove, tapping his staff now and then against the dry clods at his feet. In his other hand he carries a wooden bowl, and in the girdle at his waist he has tied a bit of cloth, which he uses to rub the bowl clean after he has eaten. He is going to a place where he will be mocked and abused, where the neighbors who were once quick to offer him a bit of some choice sweet or fresh fruit now curse his name and slam their doors in his face. Sometimes he sees one of his former schoolmates dodge down a side street to avoid meeting him, or a young woman who, when he was dressed in his father's expensive finery, once smiled upon him now averts her eyes from his shabby figure as he passes by. Still he goes along cheerfully and greets everyone with pleasure, for he has not changed, only he has put off everything that constrained him, and now he is never ashamed. Smiling, gracious, always courteous, he holds out his bowl, and sooner or later someone takes pity on him, and he is provided for. "God grant you peace," he says, and the merciful person, whether stranger or friend, feels the unsettling warmth of his gratitude, so good-natured and serene.

In the town the lower streets are strangely empty, though the house fronts are open and a few sparrows fly in and out the windows. Francesco looks about uncertainly for signs of life, a hand hanging wash out of a window, the sound of laughter behind an unopened door, but there is nothing. Both hunger and curiosity gnaw at him as he makes his way up the streets of his childhood. He knows every turning, every shortcut, the entrance and egress of every flight of stone steps. He avoids, as he always does now, the narrow passageway to his father's house, turning instead toward the church of Santa Maria. Raised voices come to him from the square before the bishop's palace, and he hastens toward them. Two men are there, arguing over a pair of shoes, each holding one and refusing to give it up to the other. Francesco calls out to them, but they are too absorbed in their quarrel to be distracted.

He hears footsteps approaching from behind and turns to find one of his father's dyers, an old fellow, stooped and half blind from the years he has spent among the poisonous boiling kettles, shuffling toward the square, his purple-stained hands held out before him to help him find his way. When he is very close, Francesco addresses him politely. At once the old man reaches out to seize the arm Francesco offers him. "It is our young lord," he cries, grinning up at him and showing his teeth and gums, which are stained the same deep purple as his hands. "Our young lord who has gone off from us."

But he is not gone, Francesco explains, as everyone can see, he is here, but where is everyone so that they may see it?

The dyer cannot follow the sense of this jest, but he recognizes the humorous intent, and he laughs heartily. They are all, he replies, everyone who can go, at the church of San Rufino to see the chastising of a penitent whose sin is so awful he must wander the earth and go to all the holy shrines to beg for punishment and then for mercy.

Francesco leads the man a few steps into the shade of a bay tree, for the sun grows hotter by the moment. What is this crime? he inquires, and who has sent the poor sinner abroad on such a pilgrimage?

It is the Lord Pope Innocent's own decree, the dyer replies, and he throws one hand out before him, as if the Lord Pope were standing there as they speak. And the crime is this, that the man has killed and eaten his own child and killed his own wife too, though he did not eat her.

Francesco gasps and passes his arm across the old man's shoulder to protect him from the horror of what he has just said. The dyer clings to him, wheezing, his clouded eyes rolled up in their sockets. The arguing men are walking off past the bishop's house, each still clutching one useless shoe; their angry voices grow more and more faint. A dog comes out from a side street and lumbers into the square. His fur is thin, uneven, and the flesh shows through in patches, red and raw. He throws himself down near the two men, who stand in the shade of the tree, and begins gnawing a bad patch on his left hind leg.

The crowd at the church is restrained. They fill all the available space, pressed close against one another across the square and up the long incline to the passageway at one side. Most of them can't see anything, but they are not complaining. They have heard the pope's letter read out by the priest, which explains how this man, this Roberto, came to commit his crime when he was a prisoner of the Saracens, and how he has tearfully confessed and begged a penance from the Holy See. Some shoving and a few shouts of dismay arise when the time comes for the penitent to remove his tunic and kneel before the priest. Those in the front cry out—He is like a skeleton—He is covered in sores and blood—Surely he will not survive this penance—and those behind respond with questions—Does he weep?—Does he protest?—Does he try to cover his nakedness? As the first blow is struck, a woman on the upper road whimpers to her neighbor, "He has fallen," and another near her wails, "May God have mercy on his soul." Then the crowd falls silent, and the sharp report of the blows fills the air, again and again. Every ear strains to hear the sighs and groans of the penitent. They seem to come from far away, as if angels brooding over the scene were moved to see it. The knight, who has accompanied the penitent, stands facing the crowd before the smaller side door of the church, his hand resting on a stone griffin. The old priest who was so eager to carry the news remains in the darkened alcove of the central doors, his hands clutching each other, his eyes wide, fixed on the grisly scene.

On the stones, in the bright sun, Father Bernabo bends over the prostrate body of the naked man, who quivers beneath the blows. At the start he was on his knees, then he fell forward upon his hands, but now he lies flat, his arms and legs spread wide, his face turned away from the crowd. His tormentor pauses to push back his sleeves and, as he does, he looks into the faces pressing in upon him. They present a panoply of emotions: curiosity, terror, pity, hatred, jealousy, righteousness, carnal excitement, murderous passion, all on open display, as if they had taken off their daily masks and these were the true faces underneath, all motionless and breathless with anticipation. They will never see themselves as he sees them in that moment. Will he stop the punishment, or will he go on? He raises his hand to shield his eyes from the sun, looking out over the mob. There, beyond the crowd, on the Via San Rufino, he can see two men walking unhurriedly: a hermit with his staff tucked under one arm like a sword and, leaning on his arm, an old man who slows him down, pointing this way and that, his grizzled head tilted toward the hermit in the listening attitude of the blind, though he is not listening but talking incessantly. They look an odd couple, jaunty, absorbed in each other, unconcerned with the gruesome spectacle ahead. Father Bernabo looks down at the bloody rod in his hands, the broken, bleeding body at his feet. He has recognized the hermit, it is Pietro Bernardone's son, who has renounced the world. The priest bends down to touch the wet cheek of the penitent, and the blood on his fingers mixes with the man's tears and sweat, running off in a thin red stream down his face and into his beard. Then, as the crowd grows anxious, and angry voices rise up protesting the pause in the entertainment, the priest gets down on his hands and knees. He brings his mouth close to the man's ear, and says softly, "Come, Roberto. Let me help you up now. We will go into the church together."

A Rich Young Man on the Road

*When you stop on the street and give something to a
beggar, why do you always do so as quickly and
inconspicuously as possible?*

—MAX FRISCH
Questionnaire

In the morning, when he leaves Foligno, his horse knows they are on the last leg of their journey and plods along at a steady pace, requiring neither guidance nor urging. Francesco is in no hurry, for his home has none of the charms of the adventure he brings to a close with his return. Everyone will want to hear about what he has seen; even his father will listen to his descriptions of Roma, the city of wonders, of the towers and bridges, the palace of the Laterano, and all the shrines and sacred relics he visited. But he will not mention the event that most fired his imagination, because anyone who hears of it will say it was a shameful, foolish exploit, the folly of a wealthy and useless young man who hasn't the sense to appreciate his position. Suppose, his father would exclaim, just suppose some neighbor from Assisi had recognized him. How could he hold his head up in the town?

For some time, something has been coming to Francesco. He cannot be sure what it is or when it began, but he can feel it moving toward him, gathering momentum. His dreams are full of triumph; voices counsel him, showing him scenes of great glory with a promise: All this will be yours. But when he is awake there are no triumphs, though he is free to indulge himself in whatever pursuits and amusements his father's money can buy. He might decide to arrange a feast or organize a singing group or, on a feast day when his father has no use for him in the stalls, he might walk into the countryside and explore the woods and streams, the various caverns in which, as a boy, he searched for hidden treasure. Nothing obstructs him, no one contradicts him. If he says he wants to be a knight, he is encouraged at every turning and provided with armor; arrangements are made for him to join a noble party, though his parents must know, he knows, that he has neither the health nor skill at arms for such a venture. When he made up his mind to visit the holy places in Roma, he received no objections. His mother provided him with a pouch full of bread and sweets, his father offered the better of their horses, and both parents made sure that his clothes were the finest and that he carried enough silver to make proper offerings at the shrines.

His horse shakes his head as if to remind him that he has at least some small obligations as a rider, and he comes to himself with a start. It is a spring day of stunning perfection; the air is cool and fresh, the sky overhead as blue as the mantle of the Holy Virgin, and on either side of the road, the fields stretch away pleasantly, olive trees on one side, grain on the other, bordered by ranks of cypress and pine. There are contingents of chaffinches chirping in the smoky leaves of the olive trees and swallows whirling overhead in undulating formations, like fallen leaves in a stream. He passes two peasants digging mud from the side of the road and another leading a reluctant goat by a bit of dirty rope. They glance at him as he goes by, a rich young man, carefree, and they give terse responses to his friendly salutations, for they have work to do and cannot ride about the countryside dressed like a fop on a fine horse. The goat makes a strangled cry, struggling at the end of his rope while his owner curses and threatens him, swearing he will not live another day. Francesco looks away, wounded as he always is by displays of pointless ferocity. He has seen too many in the last few days, especially in the city, where men and beasts are crowded together and tempers flare at the most innocent remark. At the Basilica of San Pietro he saw two men fighting on the very steps, and later, when he came out, there was such a quantity of blood— though no sign of the combatants—that he thought one had surely killed the other. And it was there, as he stood looking about nervously, that a voice called to him from the shadows of the vestibule and the peculiar and wonderful adventure began.

"Have you given it all to the thieving priests?" the voice

inquired. "Or isn't there a coin to spare for those that may truly have need of it?"

Francesco stepped away from the blood soaking into the paving stones and approached the man, if he was a man, for all he could see was one bare foot, so swollen and bruised it looked more like a rotten vegetable than human flesh. "I have not given it all," he said, stepping in under the arch. He could see nothing, for the daylight had dazzled his eyes and now the shadows confounded them, but he heard the harsh laughter of several men. One of them said, "Here is the last honest man in the world," and another responded, "It proves what I have been telling you, that the judgment day is near, for here is the new Christ among us to prove it."

"And the pope is the Antichrist," the first speaker declared. Francesco gazed down as his eyes became accustomed to the dark. There were three of them; two were old fellows, the third, the one who had announced the imminence of the judgment day, was a youth of perhaps Francesco's age with thick blond hair, scarcely any beard, and an open, ingenuous expression. He looked Francesco up and down with a bold, rapacious eye. "Now that's a fine cloak such as only a nobleman could afford," he observed.

"I am not a nobleman," Francesco replied. "But my father is a cloth merchant."

The young man got to his feet awkwardly, pressing his hands behind him against the wall. When he was halfway up, he lurched forward onto his one good leg. The other was stunted and shriveled, the muscles in the calf atrophied, the skin tight against the bone. He could put his weight on this leg long enough to make a hopping step. He crossed the space to Francesco with a rolling, out-of-kilter gait, then propped himself against the other wall. "Wouldn't I look a prince in such a cloak as that?" he said, smiling up into Francesco's face. He was missing the lower teeth on the right side of his face, and when he smiled his lower lip fell in over the gap.

"For the love of God," said one of the old men, "give us a coin if you won't give us the cloak."

Francesco turned, narrowing his eyes to make out the speaker, crouched beside his friend, who rubbed his face with his palms and echoed, "Yes, give us a coin, for the love of God."

"For the love of God," Francesco said.

In the church he had seen the faithful crowded around the tomb of the apostle Pietro. As the pilgrims arrived at the rail, each one placed a coin on the stone ledge and said a brief prayer. Francesco was shocked by the paltriness of these contributions. Many of these people were dressed in the best silks, woolens, and furs, their fingers and throats covered in jewels, even the clasps on their girdles made of beaten gold, but when it came time to make an offering in the name of the apostle who was chosen by Christ to protect his church, who had been his closest companion, the witness of his crucifixion and triumph over death, who was himself crucified in this very place and gave up his life willingly in the cause of his faith, then these wealthy men and women dug into their purses and came up with a single coin. What could account for such stinginess? Did they think the Son of God was a beggar who would be grateful for their narrow charity? Did his sublime sacrifice require no more repayment than this? When Francesco's turn came, he opened his purse, took out a handful of coins, and scattered them across the stones, where they rolled and spun and slipped through the rail, clattering on the tomb. The other pilgrims turned to stare at him, and he glared back proudly, though he did not speak his reproving thoughts. Then he strode out through the crowd without looking back.

Outside, he had found the bloody steps, and then these beggars called to him, claiming whatever he had left "for the love of God."

Francesco gazed into the eager eyes of the young man who seemed to imagine no greater glory than to have such a cloak. "Will you trade your clothes for mine?" he said. For reply the youth gave a hoot of delight. The old men cackled together; here was an odd business. "Will you let me sit here with you?" Francesco continued as he pulled off his cloak, his doublet, his leather girdle. The young man began stripping off his rags, which took no time at all, as he had only a short sackcloth tunic and a pair of filthy breeches embroidered with holes. "I will have to take my other clothes back when I go," Francesco explained, examining the contents of his purse, "but I will leave you my cloak and all but two of these coins; I will need that much for my journey home."

"Giuseppe is right," one of the old men remarked. "This proves God's judgment is nigh on this world."

Francesco laughed. He was half naked, bent over to pull off his leggings. Giuseppe had already donned his shirt. "And will you share your food with me?" he added. This set them all into laughter. "Oh yes," they agreed. Giuseppe slid down the wall to the stones, clutching his new cloak, which he had bundled in his arms like a baby. "You are welcome to everything we have," he announced, with the casual grace and courtesy of a lord offering hospitality to some bedraggled traveler who has arrived at his door after days of wandering.

So Francesco stayed with them all day, and everyone who saw him assumed he was a beggar. He experienced the most thrilling and exotic sensations, he who had always been admired and envied in his own town. Even when he was taken prisoner and shoved into a black cell in Perugia, he had been treated respectfully and lodged with the nobility, because the Perugians knew his father was rich and would pay a heavy ransom for his release. Now he was an object of derision, the butt of cruel jokes. The passing crowd never stopped mocking the company in the vestibule, calling them thieves and felons and complaining that their presence fouled the pure air of the holy shrine. "For the love of God," Francesco pleaded with his hand out, and he saw contempt in the faces of all who heard him, even in those who vouchsafed to toss him a coin. It was a mystery, impenetrable and tantalizing. By changing his clothes and taking these low fellows as his companions, he was himself entirely altered. He would not, he knew, even admit to his own name, for to do so would be to shame his father, who was proud, who held his head high and believed his son to be one of the many excellent products of his own industry and business acumen.

What was this sensation, so delicious and unexpected, when a lady paused to look down at him with a haughty yet pitying eye? As he stretched out his hand to her, she turned away, drawing her skirt in close, lest he should touch it. Did she thank heaven no son of hers would ever be found in such disgraceful circumstances? And what would she say if she knew this importuning beggar was a sham, deserving neither charity nor pity, for he had a horse, a purse, fine clothes, and would return in a day or two to his father's comfortable house, where a servant would greet him at the door?

When evening came, two more men joined the group, and they all sat down in the street to share the food they had begged. It was poor stuff, black bread and a little grain which they made into a porridge, for one of them possessed an iron pot and another had begged some sticks of firewood. Francesco listened to their lively conversation, full of profanity and derision for the vanity of the world. Though he was wealthy, they included him, as if he, too, did not know when he would find a meal again. After they had eaten, he changed back into his own clothes and laughed with them over the miracle of his transformation. Yet he felt an aching premonitory sadness as the linen settled across his shoulders: it was as though he was putting on a costume that would deceive only a fool, for a wise man would see at once that it did not suit him, that it must belong to some other man, an elegant, stylish young man, and that Francesco, in his own clothes, was an impostor. He folded the cloak and laid it in Giuseppe's lap, accepting his enthusiastic blessing and the boisterous farewells of the others who promised him their hospitality whenever he should return.

Then, bowing and waving as they repeatedly called out his name, he wandered into the dark streets alone.

Now he is himself again, but not himself; something has changed, and the world looks different because of it. He has acquired, among other novelties, a memory he will not share. His horse carries him back over the same road he traveled. His senses are open; he is prey to sudden and conflicting emotions; he sees himself from the outside, and he is not entirely gratified by what he sees.

His back is stiff and sore from days of riding and from the long rounds of the shrines. He shrugs, attempting to shake out the soreness, and rolls his head in a slow circle, easing the knotted muscles in his neck. As he does this, his horse starts, making a panicked sidestep that nearly unseats him. He catches up the reins as he lifts himself out of the saddle, then, when he drops back into his seat, he loosens his knees, gripping the horse's flanks with his calves. He knows as he goes through these automatic calming responses that there is something in the road just ahead, something that was not there a moment ago. The horse comes to a standstill in a cloud of dust that rises to his knees, and he stands working his head back and forth against the bit. Francesco rests a hand upon his mane and says his name softly, reassuring him as he looks down past the foaming lips to see what has so terrified this normally reliable creature.

The leper stands in the middle of the road, perfectly still. One hand rests on the bell cord around his neck, the other hangs limply at his side. He is dressed in a filthy garment, patched together from bits of sacking and undyed wool, which hangs loosely upon his emaciated body. He regards Francesco and the horse steadily, his head slightly turned and his chin lifted, the better to see them, for his disease has eaten away half of his face and he has only one eye.

Francesco does not speak, he cannot move. They face each other on the road, and the sun pours down over them, so that there are no shadows anywhere, nothing to soften or dim the reality of this encounter and nowhere to hide from the necessity of playing it out. The leper's eye drills into Francesco; he can feel it penetrating into his brain. From childhood he has had a horror of lepers, and he has always avoided the *laʒaretto* at the foot of Mount Subasio, where they sometimes congregate in the road, ringing their bells and calling out for alms. The stench rising from their rotting flesh, their grotesque faces, their phlegmy, guttural voices, pursue him in dreams, from which he wakes sweating and shouting for help.

But this is no dream, and there is no point in shouting now, for no one will hear. He glances back down the road and into the neat ranks of the olive trees. The world is uncommonly still. Even the birds have been silenced, frightened, no doubt, by the brief commotion of the horse.

He could ride on. There is no reason to stop. As he passes, he can throw down his last coin to the leper. His horse lifts one hoof and paws the dirt. It is time to go on, to go home. As Francesco drops his hand to the reins, his eyes fall upon his own expensive, well-fitting glove, and it dawns on him that this leper is not wearing gloves, which is odd; he and his kind are required to wear them when they leave their hospitals, just as they are required to wear and ring their bells to warn the unwary traveler of their approach.

Again Francesco looks down upon the solitary figure of the leper, who has not moved a muscle. His hand is still wrapped about the cord of the bell, his head arrested at an angle. He is like a weatherbeaten statue, and Francesco has the sense that he has been standing there, in his path, forever.

Something has been coming toward him, or he has been coming to something; he has known this for some time, and he has bent his energy in the direction of finding out what it might be. This was the reason for his pilgrimage to Roma. At the shrines he recited the requisite prayers, gazed upon the relics, bones, bits of hair and cloth, vials of blood and tears, profferred the proper offerings, but he did not feel the burden of his sins lifted, and this spiritual restlessness drove him on. Only when he was with the beggars beneath the portico at the basilica did he feel some respite from this condition of urgent expectancy.

He is in the grip of it again as he swings one leg over the saddle and drops to the ground beside his horse. The stillness of the world makes every sound acute: the clinking of the bridle chain as he leads the animal to a green patch nearby, the sound of grass tearing, and then the big jaws grinding as the horse chews the first clump. Francesco runs his hands through his hair, bats the dust from the front of his surcoat, and turns to face the man, who is there, waiting for him.

The leper watches him with interest. His blasted face is bathed in sunlight; the black hole that was his eye has a steely sheen, and a few moist drops on his lips glitter like precious stones. He moves at last, releasing his bell cord and extending his hand slowly, palm up, before him.

This supplicating gesture releases Francesco, for it dictates the countergesture, which he realizes he longs to make. Without hesitation, he strides across the distance separating him from his obligation, smiling all the while as if stepping out to greet an old and dear friend. He opens his purse, extracts the thin piece of silver inside it, and closes it up again. He is closer now than he has ever been to one of these unfortunate beings, and the old familiar reaction of disgust and nausea rises up, nearly choking him, but he battles it down. He can hear the rasp of the leper's diseased, difficult breath, rattling and wet. The war between Francesco's will and his reluctance overmasters him; he misses a step, recovers, then drops to one knee before the outstretched hand, which is hardly recognizable as a hand but is rather a lumpish, misshapen thing, the fingers so swollen and callused that they are hardly differentiated, the flesh as hard as an animal's rough paw. Carefully, Francesco places his coin in the open palm, where it glitters, hot and white. For a moment he tries to form some simple speech, some pleasantry that will restore him to the ordinary world, but even as he struggles, he understands that this world is gone from him now, that there is no turning back; it was only so much smoke, blinding and confusing him, but he has come through it somehow, he has found the source of it, and now, at last, he is standing in the fire. Tenderly he takes the leper's hand, tenderly he brings it to his lips. At once his mouth is flooded with an unearthly sweetness, which pours over his tongue, sweet and hot, burning his throat and bringing sudden tears to his eyes. These tears moisten the corrupted hand he presses to his mouth. His ears are filled with the sound of wind, and he can feel the wind chilling his face, a cold, harsh wind blowing toward him from the future, blowing away everything that has come before this moment, which he has longed for and dreaded, as if he thought he might not live through it. He reaches up, clinging to the leper's tunic, for the wind is so strong, so cold, he fears he cannot stand against it. Behind him, the horse lifts his head from his grazing and lets out a long, impatient whinny, but Francesco does not hear him. He is there in the road, rising to his feet, and the leper assists him, holding him by the shoulders. Then the two men clutch each other, their faces pressed close together, their arms entwined. The sun beats down, the air is hot and still, yet they appear to be caught in a whirlwind. Their clothes whip about; their hair stands on end; they hold on to each other for dear life.

Notes

St. Francis's first biographer was the Franciscan friar Thomas of Celano, of whom little is known. He entered the order sometime between 1213 and 1215 and, though he was not a member of the inner circle, he was acquainted with the founder. Celano was well educated and wellborn, and soon rose to prominence in the order. He authored a life of St. Clare and is traditionally believed to have written the liturgical sequence *Dies Irae*.

In 1221, according to Jordan of Giano, Celano was sent to Germany to found an order in Augsburg. By 1222 he was *custos* of Mainz, Worms, Cologne, and Speer, and the following year he was appointed vicar provincial in Germany, replacing Caesar of Speyer, who was attending the general chapter in Assisi.

Sometime after this, between 1214 and 1228, Celano returned to Italy. There is no evidence that he was in Francis's company there, though he does appear to have attended the canonization ceremony on July 16, 1228, when Ugolino de Segni, patron of the order and now Pope Gregory IX, came to Assisi to declare his old friend a saint. In this same year, Gregory commissioned Celano to write an official biography of Francis. Celano delivered his manuscript, commonly referred to as the *First Life*, on February 25, 1229.

Fifteen years later, in 1244, at a general chapter held in Genoa, Celano was called upon by the newly elected minister general,

Crescentius of Jesi, to expand his original work to include new material attesting to the character, works, and miracles of St. Francis. To this end, Crescentius put out a call to all the friars to collect whatever material they could concerning the miracles and the life and to forward them to Thomas of Celano for use in his new biography. A manuscript compiled by the "three companions," Leo (Leone), Rufino, and Angelo, probably written by Leo, was delivered to Celano with a cover letter dated Greccio, August 11, 1246. This letter has survived, but, unfortunately, is not attached to the original manuscript, occasioning centuries of controversy and discussion about just which stories were in the original collection and which were added later, by accident or design, as the years passed and the saint's popularity increased.

On May 23, 1260, the general chapter of the Friars Minor in Narbonne, France, determined that a new *Legenda* or *Life* should be compiled, based on those already in existence. This task was given to the minister general of the order, Brother John of Fidanza, later St. Bonaventure. Six years later, at the general chapter held in Paris, Bonaventure's biography, *Legenda Major,* was declared the official biography of St. Francis; all other lives and histories were to be destroyed.

Bonaventure's biography is largely borrowed from Celano's, though the stories are often compressed and narrated in a more pompous, less lively style. The anecdotes taken from Celano are in no particular order, and Bonaventure often fails to mention the name of the other friars involved. His principal additions are long lists of miracles performed by St. Francis both before and after his death. The *Legenda Major* was designed to be read in the refectories of the more than fifteen hundred friaries and four hundred Poor Clares' houses then in existence.

To give some notion of the effectiveness of the Paris decree in destroying the earliest, presumably most reliable sources for St. Francis's life, we can compare the survival rates of the various manuscripts. Some four hundred copies of the *Legenda Major,* dating from thirteenth- and fourteenth-century publications, have survived. Only two copies of Celano's *Second Life*, one in Assisi and one in Marseilles, are extant, and of the *First Life*, eleven copies have survived, preserved by monks who, for whatever reason, did not obey the decree: one copy by Franciscans, eight by Cistercians, and three by Benedictines.

Celano's two *Lives* and Bonaventure's *Legenda Major* are among the early sources available to the English reader in one text, *St. Francis of Assisi: Writings and Early Biographies*, edited by Marion A. Habig. This invaluable compilation includes all the "recognized, authentic" writings of St. Francis, that is, his various Rules for the order, letters, prayers, and praises, and his final testament. In addition, the omnibus contains the three "legends," compiled for Celano's *Second Life*, which scholars now generally agree were written by Leo: *The Legend of the Three Companions, The Legend of Perugia*, and *The Mirror of Perfection*. These works are followed by the immensely popular fourteenth-century collection *The Little Flowers of St. Francis*. All references to the above-listed works in the following notes are to the Habig omnibus.

Equally useful and interesting is the *Scripta Leonis*, translated and edited by Rosalind Brooke. This text is an English translation of "all the early manuscripts of any substance" that have been identified as among the stories put together by Leo, Rufino, and Angelo, the "three companions," at the request of Crescentius of Jesi. One of the many pleasures of this book (Ms. Brooke's lucid explanation of the surviving manuscripts' complex history is another) is the arrangement of the manuscript, with the original Latin page facing each page of translation. Very little knowledge of Latin is required to appreciate the charm and simplicity of the original author's style. An example is Leo's recollection of the adjuration

St. Francis gave the nagging novice who longed for a psalter of his own: *"Postquam habueris psalterium, concupisces et uoles habere breuiarium; postquam habueris breuiarium, sedebis in cathedra tamquam magnus prelatus dicens fratri tuo: 'Apporta michi breuiarium.'"* ("After you have a psalter you will want and hanker for a breviary; after you have a breviary you will sit in an armchair like a great prelate, saying to your brother: 'Bring me my breviary.'")

The following frequently cited texts will be abbreviated in the notes as follows:

EFG *Early Franciscan Government*
NV   *Nova Vita di San Francesco*
O   *St. Francis of Assisi: Omnibus of Sources*
SL   *Scripta Leonis*
TLF *The Little Flowers of St. Francis*

Full citations for these sources will be given at the first entry. Margin numbers refer to pages in text.

INTRODUCTION

4   "This town": Rosalind B. Brooke, ed. and trans., *Scripta Leonis, Rufini et Angeli Sociorum S. Francisci* (Oxford: Clarendon Press, 1970), pp. 262–3.
5   "My Lord Bishop": "Legend of the Three Companions," in *St. Francis of Assisi, Omnibus of Sources,* ed. Marion A. Habig (Chicago: Franciscan Herald Press, 1983), pp. 908–9.
6   Fratres Minores: literally, "lesser brothers." This designation originates in the First Rule of 1221, "and let them be lesser brothers." Celano adds, "and when these words were spoken, indeed in that same hour, he said: 'I wish that this fraternity should be called the Order of Friars Minor.'" 1 Celano 38 in O, p. 260.

6   Within a few years: Adolf Holl, *The Last Christian,* trans. Peter Heinegg (New York: Doubleday, 1980), p. 126.

6   the *custos* and ministers: "In time, provinces were divided into custodies, while the title 'custos' came to be used not as an alternative to 'Provincial Minister' but for the administrative officer of the custody." John Moorman, *A History of the Franciscan Order* (Oxford: Oxford University Press, 1968), p. 62.

7   Francesco died peacefully: His final illness was a complex dysfunction affecting his stomach, liver, and diaphragm. He suffered frequent hemorrhages and, near the end, developed edema. Some scholars speculate that he had tuberculosis, as his hemorrhages, recurrent fevers, and reputation for sleeplessness and spectacular bouts of energy suggest. His eye disease, contracted in Syria, is usually diagnosed as trachoma. See Holl, pp. 201–2.

9   St. Columban: For an authoritative discussion of the stories about St. Francis and various animals, see Edward Armstrong, *Saint Francis: Nature Mystic* (Berkeley: University of California Press, 1973).

10   "one habit, quilted": The original habit of the Fratres Minores was gray, not brown, and the Franciscans were sometimes called "gray friars," as distinguished from the Dominicans or Friars Preachers, who were called "black friars." For a discussion of the formalization of the habit, see Cajetan Esser, *Origins of the Franciscan Order* (Chicago: Franciscan Herald Press, 1970), pp. 96–104.

10   at Assisi, and Brother Elia: Much has been written about Brother Elia of Cortona. He joined the order somewhere between 1211 and 1215; that is, early on. He was well educated, had been a teacher, and had studied law in Bologna. In 1217, when the Fratres Minores expanded to the east, St. Francis chose Elia as the first minister there. He was highly successful in this post, founding friaries at Acre, Damietta, and Constantinople. Shortly before St. Francis died, he appointed Elia minister general of the order. St.

Francis was very ill at this time, and he seems to have relied upon Elia to supervise his care.

Elia's generalship was a disaster, and he was eventually deposed by Pope Gregory IX, in response to complaints throughout the order. Brother Elia is sometimes seen in the role of Judas to St. Francis's Christ, and indeed it is difficult to understand how he could have been so entirely under the influence of St. Francis's personality when he clearly had so little sympathy for his ideals. For a complete discussion of the character and generalship of Brother Elia, see Rosalind Brooke, *Early Franciscan Government* (London: Cambridge University Press, 1959).

10 In September 1230: See O, pp. 67–70, also Moorman, pp. 89–92.

11 From the very start: It starts in Celano, with mild carping about the brothers who disappoint the holy father and descriptions of St. Francis's frustration at the pope's insistence that he rewrite the Rule. Paul Sabatier, in his famous 1894 biography, suggests that all saints are, by their nature, in revolt against church authority. "The priest of the thirteenth century is the antithesis of the saint, he is almost always his enemy." Paul Sabatier, *Life of St. Francis of Assisi,* trans. Louise Seymour Houghton (New York: Scribners, 1938), p. XIV.

11 My brief account of the twelfth- and thirteenth-century poverty movements in Europe derives from several sources, including: Norman Cohn, *The Pursuit of the Millennium* (New York: Oxford University Press, 1970); G. G. Coulton, *The Medieval Scene* (Cambridge: Cambridge University Press, 1967); Rosalind Brooke, *The Coming of the Friars* (New York: Harper and Row, 1975); and Edward Armstrong.

NIGHT IN THE FOREST

18 The trip from Siena to Assisi is described in Arnoldo Fortini, *Nova Vita di San Francesco,* trans. Helen Moax (New York: Cross-

road, 1980), pp. 581–96; SL, pp. 116–17; 1 Celano 105, in O, pp. 319–21; and Omer Englebert, *St. Francis of Assisi* (Ann Arbor, Mi.: Servant Books, 1979), pp. 257–60.

26 sitting on the floor: The *Scripta Leonis* says Brother Benedict of Piratro took the dictation of Francesco's final testament. SL, pp. 116–17.

26 "This is how": In his final testament, St. Francis stressed the importance to him of the order's maintenance as strictly mendicant, without property, either communal or personal. The following selections from this testament are quoted in O, pp. 67–70:

> When God gave me some friars, there was no one to tell me what I should do; but the Most High himself made it clear to me that I must live the life of the Gospel. I had this written down briefly and simply and his holiness the Pope confirmed it for me. Those who embraced this life gave everything they had to the poor. They were satisfied with one habit which was patched inside and outside, and a cord, and trousers. We refused to have anything more.

The testament concludes with a charge that leaves no doubt as to Francesco's deathbed lucidity.

> The friars should not say, this is another Rule. For this is a reminder, admonition, exhortation, and my testament which I, Brother Francis, worthless as I am, leave to you, my brothers, that we may observe in a more Catholic way the Rule we have promised to God. The Minister General and all the other ministers and custodes are bound in virtue of obedience not to add anything to these words or subtract from them. They should always have this writing with

them as well as the Rule and at the chapters they hold, when the Rule is read, they should read these words also.

In virtue of obedience, I strictly forbid any of my friars, clerics or lay brothers, to interpret the Rule or these words, saying, "This is what they mean." God inspired me to write the Rule and these words plainly and simply, and live by them, doing good to the last.

29   "Bring some ashes": Englebert, p. 273.

ELIA'S JOYFUL MESSAGE

32   To Brother Gregory: This is the full text of the letter Brother Elia sent to Brother Gregory, the provincial minister of the Fratres Minores in France. It was, doubtless, sent to other ministers. Only one manuscript copy has survived. See O, pp. 1955–60.

ELIA CLOSES THE DOOR

38   For a summary of the plot to hide St. Francis's body, see NV, p. 62n; also EFG, pp. 137–43.

38   even Jean of Brienne: Moorman, p. 86.

38   called in ancient times: EFG, p. 138.

39   "All you need now is wives": Quoted in EFG, p. 150.

40   It would be better: See EFG, p. 142, for a description of the dangers a prospective saint's corpse ran in transportation to the grave.

42   For six hundred years: The grave of St. Francis was not discovered until 1818. See Holl, p. 219.

A CONVALESCENT

46   For St. Francis's stay at San Damiano, see SL, pp. 162–7.

48   They do the bidding: For an account of Brother Elia's char-

acter and the rumors circulated about him in the order, see EFG, pp. 83–105.

48   "For she is useful": Following is the full text of "The Canticle of Brother Sun," translated by Benen Fahy in O, pp. 130–1. The stanza praising God for those who grant pardon was added sometime after the preceding verses, when the podesta and the bishop of Assisi were embroiled in a feud that threatened to wreck the peace of the city. St. Francis was too sick to get up from the floor, but he sent a few friars to sing the revised canticle at an assembly in the town square attended by the two intransigent officials. At the conclusion of the singing, the podesta burst into tears, fell at the bishop's feet, and said, "See, I am ready to give satisfaction to you in everything, just as you please." The bishop confessed himself "by nature, quick tempered," begged the podesta to make allowances for him, and the quarrel was resolved. See SL, p. 169.

The last stanza in praise of Sister Death was composed when the saint was on his deathbed.

THE CANTICLE OF BROTHER SUN

Most high, all-powerful, all good, Lord!
    All praise is yours, all glory, all honour
    and all blessing.
To you, alone, Most High, do they belong.
    No mortal lips are worthy
    To pronounce your name.
All praise be yours, my Lord, through all that you have
        made,
    And first my lord Brother Sun,
    Who brings the day; and light you give to us through
        him.
How beautiful is he, how radiant in all his splendour!
    Of you, Most High, he bears the likeness.

All praise be yours, my Lord, through Sister Moon and
      Stars;
  In the heavens you have made them, bright
  and precious and fair.
All praise be yours, my Lord, through Brothers Wind and
      Air,
  And fair and stormy, all the weather's moods,
  By which you cherish all that you have made.
All praise be yours, my Lord, through Sister Water,
  So useful, lowly, precious and pure.
All praise be yours, my Lord, through Brother Fire,
  Through whom you brighten up the night,
  How beautiful is he, how gay! Full of power and
     strength.
All praise be yours, my Lord, through Sister Earth, our
      mother,
  Who feeds us in her sovereignty and produces
  Various fruits with coloured flowers and herbs.
All praise be yours, my Lord, through those who grant
     pardon
  For love of you; through those who endure
  Sickness and trial.
  Happy those who endure in peace,
  By you, Most High, they will be crowned.
All praise be yours, my Lord, through Sister Death,
  From whose embrace no mortal can escape.
Woe to those who die in mortal sin!
  Happy those She finds doing your will!
  The second death can do no harm to them.
Praise and bless my Lord, and give him thanks,
  And serve him with great humility.

A VISIT TO THE DOCTOR

52   St. Francis's medical treatment is described in SL, pp. 172–5; also 1 Celano 99–101, in O, pp. 313–16.

54   gold and coral spoons: for a description of medieval flatware, see Norbert Elias, *The Civilizing Process* (New York: Urizen Books, 1978), pp. 67–8.

BROTHER BODY WINS THE DAY

58   "He finds": The persuasive friar is quoted in 2 Celano 210–11, in O, pp. 530–1.

A MOUNTAIN STORM

71   the wounds: For the events surrounding the stigmatization of St. Francis, see "The Considerations of the Holy Stigmata," in *The Little Flowers of St. Francis of Assisi*, trans. and ed. Raphael Brown (New York: Doubleday, 1958), pp. 170–216.

WHAT IS AN EYE

74   For St. Francis's response to the curious friar, see 2 Celano 125–6, in O, p. 472.

BROTHER LEONE IS TRANSPORTED

80   For Brother Leone's response to the wounds of St. Francis, see "The Considerations of the Holy Stigmata," in TLF, p. 194.

WILD MEN AND AN EMPEROR

86 Scolding the emperor is described in 1 Celano 43, in O, p. 264. The emperor was Otto IV, whose reign was indeed a short one. He was excommunicated by Innocent III in 1211. See Englebert, p. 78.

86 frightened by wild men: "So assimilated to their woodland haunts did Francis and his companions appear that women fled from them and folk spoke of them as . . . *quasi silvestres homines.*" Armstrong, p. 24, see also 2 Celano 63, in which the beds of the friars are described as "like the lairs of wild beasts."

88 *"Miserere mei"*: Psalm 51.

89 *pavesari:* soldiers who protected crossbowmen with shields between shots. Philippe Contamine, *War in the Middle Ages*, trans. Michael Jones (Cambridge: Blackwell, 1994), p. 73.

AN IMPORTUNATE NOVICE

94 For an account of the persistent novice, see SL, pp. 208–17.

A FRIAR DAMNED

100 The story of Brother Elia's damnation is found in TLF, pp. 128–30. It does not appear in the earliest sources and may well have been fabricated after Elia was denounced and excommunicated. It also appears in Julien Green's biography, *God's Fool*, trans. Peter Heinegg (New York: Harper and Row, 1985), pp. 247–9. Rosalind Brooke disputes its validity in EFG, pp. 100–1.

BROTHER FIRE DESIRES A BLANKET

108 For St. Francis's refusal to help put out the fire, see SL, pp. 176–9.

108 the count: This count was Orlando of Chiusi, who ceded Mount La Verna to the friars on September 8, 1218. See TLF, p. 344.
109 Rufino recalls: St. Francis's care of the starving friar is described in SL, pp. 88–91.

DEMONS IN A TOWER

114 For an account of St. Francis and the demons, see SL, pp. 248–53.
115 toads into his mouth: see NV, p. 54. Fortini's description of thirteenth-century torture concludes: "teeth were wrenched out, toads stuffed in their mouths. Cremona interred its prisoners . . . reduced to quenching their thirst with oil from lamps and eating the cadavers of their companions . . . in Mantua . . . 3,000 inhabitants had their noses cut off."

A SNOW FAMILY

120 The story of St. Francis and the snow family is in 2 Celano 116–17, in O, pp. 458–9.

AT THE HARBOR

128 The gray friars: The friars "set sail on June 24, 1219, St. John's Day, and first put into port at the island of Cyprus. They reached St. John d'Acre about the middle of July, and a few days later Damietta in the Nile Delta, which had been under siege by the crusaders for a year." Englebert, p. 174. Fortini suggests that the friars left from an Apulian port, Barletta, Bari, or Brindisi, the standard route crusaders took to the east. See Fortini, p. 395.
128 plain barks and galleys: See Simon Lloyd, "The Crusading Movement, 1096–1274," in Jonathan Riley-Smith, *The Oxford Illustrated History of the Crusades* (New York: Oxford University

Press, 1995), pp. 58–65; also Harry W. Hazard, ed., *The Art and Architecture of the Crusader States* (Madison: University of Wisconsin Press, 1977), pp. 36–68.

129 The French knights: The Fifth Crusade was called by Innocent III at the Lateran Council in 1215, which St. Francis probably attended. Innocent set June 1, 1217, as the date when the crusaders would set sail from Brindisi and Messina for the Holy Land. When Innocent died suddenly the following year, his successor, Honorius III, proved equally committed to the Crusade, but the enormity of the task, which involved organizing and transporting men and equipment from all over Europe, defeated his resolve, and the Crusade dragged on until 1221, ending in humiliating defeat for the crusaders, who failed even to acquire the true cross, which, it turned out, Sultan al-Kamil did not have.

The failure was in good part due to the reluctance of Emperor Frederick II, who did not set sail from Cyprus until 1228. Frederick was a fabulous personage, called by his contemporaries the "Stupor Mundi" and "the Hammer of the World." He was a Norman, raised in Umbria and Sicily as a ward of Pope Innocent III (he was baptized in the same church as St. Francis), intelligent, multilingual, much interested in mathematics and philosophy, acquainted with and respectful of the Muslim religion. Like St. Francis, Frederick was always traveling, but he did not travel lightly. His entourage included a harem, elephants, camels, falcons, a guard of Lucera Saracens, Arab, Greek, and Jewish attendants, doctors and scientists, his crown, his jewels, and a good part of his extensive library. See Thomas F. Madden, *A Concise History of the Crusades* (Lanham, Md.: Rowman & Littlefield, 1999), pp. 143–65.

129 "I cannot choose among you": For St. Francis's method of choosing his companions, see Englebert, p. 174.

130 *crucesignato:* The word "crusade" is not a medieval term. It comes from the word *"crucesignati,"* which means "those signed by the cross."

"Each crusader joined the enterprise by taking a pilgrim's vow. During that 'taking of the cross,' or 'crossing,' a crusader swore to make a pilgrimage to the Holy Sepulcher, the tomb in which Christ was laid and from which he rose. Because of the great expense and difficulties of such a journey, a crusader received a remission from sins, just as would a pilgrim who traveled to a holy shrine. As a pilgrim, a crusader's lands and properties were placed under the protection of the church until his return. The crusader's vow was frequently accompanied by other vows of fasting or abstention from sex or by special devotions to be performed during the course of the pilgrimage. Finally, a simple cross was sewn onto the shoulder of the crusader's garment to signify his status as a pilgrim." Madden, pp. 1–10.

"During their absence crusaders would be exempt from all taxes, secular or ecclesiastical, and from the paying of any interest to the Jews." Anthony Mockler, *Francis of Assisi: The Wandering Years* (Oxford: Phaidon Press, 1976), p. 206.

GOING TO MEET THE SULTAN

134   For St. Francis's prophecy, see 2 Celano 30, in O, pp. 388–9.

134   for the false prophet: "Invoking the 666 years of the beast of the apocalypse, he [Innocent III] saw in the completion of six hundred years since the rise of Islam a sign that Divine Providence would respond to the Christian hope for the liberation of the Holy Land." James Powell, *Anatomy of a Crusade* (Philadelphia: University of Pennsylvania Press, 1986), p. 18.

135   A company of pilgrims: For accounts of the yearlong siege of Damietta in the Fifth Crusade, see Madden, pp. 143–66; Amin Maalouf, *The Crusade Through Arab Eyes*, trans. Jon Rothschild (New York: Schocken, 1983), pp. 201–31; Powell, pp. 123–73; and Steven Runciman, *A History of the Crusades*, Vol. 3 (New York: Cambridge University Press, 1988), pp. 145–70.

135 the French blame: The cardinal was Pelagius, a Spaniard appointed papal legate by Innocent III in September 1214.

136 the Shepherd's Psalm: Psalm 23.

136 For St. Francis's meeting with al-Kamil, see Bishop Jacques de Vitry, *History of the Orient,* as quoted in O, pp. 1609–13.

137 "I went down to Marseilles": For an account of the Children's Crusade of 1212, see Runciman, pp. 139–44.

139 "syrup made from lemons": Hazard, pp. 17–18.

A MEAL IN AN EXOTIC SETTING

142 St. Francis's visit to Acre is described in Englebert, pp. 181–3.

143 He has seen a good many knights: See Jonathan Phillips, "The Latin East 1098–1291," in Jonathan Riley-Smith, pp. 112–40.

144 "If you are heading for Jerusalem": When it appeared that offering the Christians Jerusalem might be necessary to terminate the war, Sultan al-Mùassam decided to dismantle the city. See Runciman, p. 158.

145 much to the chagrin: Jacques de Vitry, at that time bishop of Acre. Bishop Vitry was a reliable chronicler of the era and an admirer of the Fratres Minores. "This order which is spreading through the whole world," he wrote, "imitates the primitive Church and the life of the Apostles in all things. Colin the Englishman, our clerk, has entered their ranks, with two others, Master Michael and Dom Matthew, to whom I had entrusted the parish of the Holy Cross. Only with difficulty do I hold back the Chanter and Henry and others." Quoted in Englebert, pp. 175–6.

146 References to St. Francis's visit to the sultan appear in Runciman, pp. 159–60; Powell, pp. 158–9; and Maalouf, pp. 274–5 (though Maalouf points out only that there are no Arab sources for the event).

147 And this was true: See Runciman, pp. 160–6.

148 They decided to throw up a ladder: For the fall of Damietta, see Powell, pp. 158–73, and Maalouf, pp. 218–31.

Notes

A FOOL AND HIS MONEY

154 For Brother Bernard's renunciation, see 1 Celano 24 and 2 Celano 15, in O, pp. 248–49 and 374–5.

AN INTERVIEW

164 the poor men of Lyons: These were the followers of Peter Waldo, later called the Waldensians. The Paterini were originally a reform movement from Milan, but in the twelfth century, they were synonymous with the Cathars. See Brooke, *The Coming of the Friars,* pp. 71–9.
165 For St. Francis's visit to Pope Innocent III, see 1 Celano 32 and 2 Celano 16, in O, pp. 254–6 and 376–78.

A CONVOCATION OF FRIARS

170 He has arrived in Venezia: Englebert says St. Francis rested in Venice, traveled to Bologna—where he threw the friars out of a house Peter Staccia had established—then went straight to Rome to ask the pope to appoint Cardinal Ugolino as the "protector, governor and correcter" of the order. Englebert, pp. 185–6.
172 For St. Francis's curse on Brother Peter and the destruction of the stone house, see 2 Celano 57–58, in O, pp. 412–13, also TLF, pp. 310–11.
175 For St. Francis's renunciation of his ministry, see Celano 143, in O, p. 477; also SL, pp. 272–5.

INNOCENT CALLS THE FAITHFUL

178 For St. Francis at the Fourth Lateran Council, see Englebert, pp. 139–46. For the council itself, see L. Elliot Binns, *Innocent III* (Archon, 1968), pp. 164–84.
179 the forest of towers:

These towers made such an impact on the general appearance of Rome, due to their sheer numbers, that a twelfth-century visitor to the city wrote that his first impression of it when he saw it from a hill-top was of a "cornfield of towers." They were so popular because they provided a natural base from which to launch interfamily skirmishes, and in many cases might be no more than a bow-shot apart.

See Paul Hetherington, *Medieval Rome, A Portrait of the City and Its Life* (New York: St. Martin's Press, 1994), p. 39.

180 the emperor Constantine's horse: the famous bronze equestrian statue of the Emperor Marcus Aurelius, which now stands in the Capitoline Museum, was thought to be of Emperor Constantine, the first Christian emperor, and therefore appropriate to the forecourt of the Lateran Palace. See Hetherington, p. 44.

A FUNERAL, SPARSELY ATTENDED

182 An iron cage: Stocks and cages were a common medieval method of punishment. See Fortini, pp. 54–63.

183 The heavy portals stand open: "That was the day when I really understood the nothingness of earthly grandeur. Incredibly the preceding night, thieves had entered and stripped the Pope of everything of value he had on. With my own eyes I saw his half-naked body lying in the middle of the church, already smelling." Jacques de Vitry, quoted in Englebert, p. 147.

AN ESCAPE BY TORCHLIGHT

188 For Clare's residence at San Damiano, see 1 Celano 18–20, in O, pp. 243–6.

192 Does it occur to her: In a letter written in 1216, Jacques de Vitry describes the "Sisters Minor": "The women live near the cities in various hospices and refuges; they live a community life

from the work of their hands, but accept no income." O, p. 1608. The Rule that Cardinal Ugolino, patron and protector of the Franciscans, gave to Clare and her disciples in 1219 provided for a regime of strict enclosure based upon the Rule of St. Benedict. "The ideal of voluntary poverty was not a male monopoly, but female mendicancy seemed unthinkable." Lawrence, p. 264.

A SERMON

194 For the sermon St. Francis preached to the Poor Ladies, see 2 Celano 207, in O, pp. 527–8.

A LAST VISIT TO THE POOR LADIES

200 For the grief of the Poor Ladies, see 1 Celano 116–18, in O, pp. 330–2.
203 *"Educ de custodia"*: Psalm 142.

IN HIDING, IN CHAINS

208 For St. Francis's persecution by his father, see 1 Celano 8–13, in O, pp. 235–40.

A LESSON FROM THE GOSPELS

216 For St. Francis's reading of the gospel lesson, see 1 Celano 21–2, in O, pp. 246–7.
218 *"Euntes autem"*: The Gospel is Matthew 10:7–10.

A PENITENT; IN THE BACKGROUND, A HERMIT

224 Innocent III composed the following fascinating document in 1203, which means the penitent Robert would have been due to return from his pilgrimage in 1206.

To the archbishops, bishops, abbots and friars to whom this letter shall come.

The bearer of this letter, Robert by name, came to the compassionate Apostolic See and tearfully confessed his sin, a great one indeed and a grave one.

For when he had been captured with his wife and daughter by the Saracens, their chief whom they call the Admiral issued an order that since a famine was imminent all those prisoners who had children should kill them; and by reason of this order the wretched man, urged on by pangs of hunger, killed and ate his daughter. And when on a second occasion another order went out, he killed his own wife; but when her flesh was cooked and served up before him, he could not bring himself to eat it.

Appalled by the horror of such a crime we have thought fit to enjoin upon him this penance; that he never hereafter on any account eat meat, and that he fast every Friday on bread and water and likewise on the Monday and Wednesday in the Lent of Christmas and the Lent of Easter; and on other days of each Lent he is to fast devoutly and remain content with one dish of pottage, observing the same on the vigils of the saints' days.

He is to go about unshod, in a woolen tunic with a very short scapular, carrying a penitent's staff a cubit in length. He is to accept no more food from anyone than suffices for a day, and he is never to spend above two nights in the same place unless driven by necessity and unable to proceed because of illness, war or weather.

In this way let him visit the shrines of the saints for three years; and when he comes to a church, let him prostrate himself and not even enter until he has received discipline with rod or whip.

He shall persist always without hope of marriage. He

shall never attend public sports. He is to say the Lord's Prayer a hundred times every day and bow the knee each time.

At the end of three years let him return with this letter to the Apostolic See to seek mercy, and take pains to observe what shall then be enjoined on him.

You, therefore, brethren and children, show pity to the pitiful and in the time of his need reveal to him the fulness of your love.

Dated at the monastery of Subiaco, the 3rd September, in the fifth year of our pontificate.

Quoted in C. R. Cheney, *Medieval Texts and Studies* (Oxford: Oxford University Press, 1973), pp. 18–19.

Penitents, alone or in groups, were not an uncommon sight on the roads of medieval Europe. Pilgrim travel from England to Rome was so frequent that guidebooks and maps were readily available, and some of these have survived the attrition of centuries. George Parks describes a variant of the route most often used in Italy made by Gerald of Bari in 1203, who, "seeking to avoid the malice of his English adversaries, made a wide circuit to reach Rome. Instead of crossing the Apennines from Parma or Bologna, he continued on to Forli and Cesna, crossing then to the headwaters of the Tiber, which he followed more or less to Assisi perhaps, and thence by the usual road to Spoleto and Rome." Parks, *The English Traveler to Italy,* pp. 190–1.

No evidence exists that the penitent Robert ever went to Assisi or that St. Francis ever saw or even heard of him. This scene is, therefore, entirely of my own devising. I have taken the liberty of placing Robert in Assisi near the end of his pilgrimage in 1206, just as Francis, a young man of twenty-four or twenty-five, was undergoing his conversion and preparing himself to embark upon a penitential journey that would last the rest of his life.

A RICH YOUNG MAN ON THE ROAD

232 For St. Francis's pilgrimage to Rome, see 2 Celano 8, in O, p. 369.

232 the shrines and sacred relics: When St. Francis visited the Basilica of St. Peter, he paid tribute to only one half of the apostle. The other half was buried in the Church of St. Paul on the outskirts of the city, and the apostle's head was in the Lateran Basilica. Also at the Lateran, according to Gerald of Bari, he could have seen "the ark of the covenant, the table of the law, the golden urn of manna, the rod of Aaron, the seven-branched candelabrum, the holy table and cloth. Here also are a tunic made by the Virgin, Christ's purple garment, two bottles of blood and water from His side, the remains of His cradle, the five loaves and two fishes, the Lord's table, and the cloth with which He wiped the feet of the apostles; in addition, the blood of John the Baptist and the ashes from his cremation and his hair-shirt; a bottle of earth from the tomb of St. John the Evangelist, and his tunic; and the heads of St. Peter and St. Paul." Quoted in Parks, p. 244.

238 The leper stands: See St. Bonaventure, *Major Life*, 5, in O, pp. 638–9.

A NOTE ON THE EARLY SOURCES

244 For a history of the "Three Companions" manuscript, see O, pp. 179–200.

244 For survival rates of Celano's *First Life* and *Second Life*, see Anthony Mockler, *St. Francis of Assisi: The Wandering Years* (Oxford: Phaidon Press, 1976), pp. 13–32.

246 *"Postquam"*: SL, p. 214.

Sources

Abulafia, David. *Frederick II: A Medieval Emperor*. London, 1992.

Aries, Philippe. *Centuries of Childhood: A Social History of Family Life*. Translated by Robert Baidick. London, 1962.

———— and Georges Duby, eds. *A History of Private Life: Revelations of the Medieval World*. Cambridge, Mass., 1988.

Armstrong, Edward. *St. Francis: Nature Mystic*. Berkeley, 1973.

Battiffol, Pierre. *History of the Roman Breviary*. Translated by Atwell M. Y. Baylay. London, 1898.

Binns, L. Elliott. *Innocent III*. 1968.

Bishop, Morris. *Saint Francis of Assisi*. Boston, 1974.

Brooke, Rosalind B. *The Coming of the Friars*. New York, 1975.

————. *Early Franciscan Government*, Cambridge, 1959.

————. *Scripta Leonis, Rufini et Angeli Sociorum S. Francisci*. Oxford, 1970.

Brown, Raphael, ed. and trans. *The Little Flowers of St. Francis of Assisi*. New York, 1958.

Cantor, Norman F. *Medieval History: The Life and Death of a Civilization*. New York, 1969.

Cheney, C. R. , ed. *Medieval Texts and Studies*. Oxford, 1973.

———— and W. H. Semple, eds. *Selected Letters of Pope Innocent III*. New York, 1953.

Chesterton, G. K. *St. Francis of Assisi*. New York, 1990.

Cioran, E. M. *Tears and Saints*. Chicago, 1995.

Cohn, Norman. *The Pursuit of the Millennium*. New York, 1970.

Contamine, Philippe. *War in the Middle Ages.* Translated by Michael Jones. Cambridge, 1994.

Coulton, G. G. *The Medieval Scene: An Informal Introduction to the Middle Ages.* Cambridge, 1967.

———. *Ten Medieval Studies.* Cambridge, 1930.

Cunningham, Lawrence S. *Saint Francis of Assisi.* Boston, 1976.

DeMause, Lloyd, ed. *The History of Childhood.* New York, 1975.

Duby, Georges. *The Early Growth of the European Economy: Warriors and Peasants.* Ithaca, 1974.

Elias, Norbert. *The Civilizing Process: The History of Manners.* New York, 1978.

Englebert, Omer. *St. Francis of Assisi.* Ann Arbor, 1979.

Erickson, Carolly. *The Medieval Vision: Essays in History and Perception.* New York, 1976.

Esser, Cajetan. *Origins of the Franciscan Order.* Translated by Aedum Daly, OFM, and Irina Lynch. Chicago, 1970.

Faure, Gabriel. *The Land of St. Francis of Assisi.* Boston, 1925.

Fortini, Arnoldo. *Francis of Assisi.* Translated by Helen Moak. New York, 1980.

Gimpel, Jean. *The Medieval Machine.* New York, 1976.

Green, Julien. *God's Fool: The Life and Times of Francis of Assisi.* Translated by Peter Heinegg. New York, 1985.

Habig, Marion, ed. *St. Francis of Assisi: Omnibus of Sources.* Chicago, 1983.

Harrison, Ted. *Stigmata.* New York, 1994.

Hazard, Harry W., ed. *The Art and Architecture of the Crusader States.* Madison, Wis., 1977.

Hetherington, Paul. *Medieval Rome: A Portrait of the City and Its Life.* New York, 1994.

Hibbert, Christopher. *Rome: The Biography of a City.* New York, 1985.

Holl, Adolf. *The Last Christian.* New York, 1980.

Hoag, John D. *Western Islamic Architecture.* New York, 1963.

Hughes, Robert. *Heaven and Hell in Western Art*. New York, 1968.

James, William. *The Varieties of Religious Experience*. New York, 1982.

Jorgenson, Johannes. *St. Francis of Assisi*. New York, 1955.

Kaftal, George. *St. Francis in Italian Painting*. London, 1980.

Kazantzakis, Nikos. *St. Francis: A Novel*. New York, 1962.

Keen, Maurice. *The Penguin History of Medieval Europe*. New York, 1968.

Klepec, Sister Elizabeth Marie, OSF, ed. *Daily Readings with St. Francis of Assisi*. Springfield, Ill., 1988.

Knowles, David, and Dimitri Obolensky. *The Middle Ages*. New York, 1968.

Lambert, M. D. *Franciscan Poverty*. London, 1961.

Lawrence, C. H. *Medieval Monasticism*. New York, 1994.

Maalouf, Amin. *The Crusade Through Arab Eyes*. Translated by Jon Rothschild. New York, 1984.

Madden, Thomas F. *A Concise History of the Crusades*. Lanham, Md.: 1999.

Mockler, Anthony. *Francis of Assisi: The Wandering Years*. Oxford, 1976.

Moore, R. I. *The Origins of European Dissent*. London, 1977.

Moorman, John. *A History of the Franciscan Order*. Oxford, 1968.

———. *St. Francis of Assisi*. London, 1982.

Mumford, Lewis. *The Myth in the Machine*. New York, 1967.

Nichols, Francis Morgan, ed. and trans. *The Marvels of Rome: Mirabilia Urbis Romae*. New York, 1986.

Origo, Iris. *The Merchant of Prato: Francesco di Marco Datini, 1335–1410*. New York, 1957.

Parks, George B., ed. *The English Traveler to Italy*. Stanford, Calif., 1954.

Peters, Edward, ed. *Heresy and Authority in Medieval Europe*. Philadelphia, 1980.

Placid, Hermann. *XIIIth Century Chronicles.* Translated by Marie-Thérèse Laureilhe. Chicago, 1961.

Powell, James M. *Anatomy of a Crusade, 1213–1221.* Philadelphia, 1986.

Riley-Smith, Jonathan. *The Crusades.* New Haven, 1987.

————, ed. *The Oxford Illustrated History of the Crusades.* Oxford, 1995.

Runciman, Steven. *A History of the Crusades.* New York, 1988.

Sabatier, Paul. *Life of St. Francis of Assisi.* Translated by Louise Seymour Houghton. New York, 1938.

Salimbene de Adam. *The Chronicle of Salimbene de Adam.* Edited by Joseph L. Baird. Binghamton, N.Y., 1986.

Setton, Kenneth M. *A History of the Crusades.* Madison, Wis., 1977.

Shaw, Henry. *Dresses and Decorations of the Middle Ages.* London, 1843.

Sticca, Sandro, ed. *Saints: Studies in Hagiography.* Binghamton, 1996.

Toaff, Ariel. *The Jews in Medieval Assisi.* Firenze, 1979.

Trexler, Richard C. *Naked Before the Father: The Renunciation of Francis of Assisi.* New York, 1989.

Von Galli, Mario, S.J. *Living Our Future: Francis of Assisi and the Church Tomorrow.* Chicago, 1972.

Villehardouin and de Joinville. *Memoirs of the Crusades.* Translated by Sir Frank T. Marzials. New York, 1958.

Walsh, Michael. *An Illustrated History of the Popes.* New York, 1980.

Watt, W. Montgomery. *The Majesty That Was Islam.* London, 1984.

A NOTE ABOUT THE AUTHOR

Valerie Martin is the author of two collections of short fic-
tion and six novels, including *Italian Fever*, *The Great
Divorce*, and *Mary Reilly*. She lived in Italy for three years
and now resides in upstate New York.

A NOTE ON THE TYPE

Pierre Simon Fournier le jeune, who designed the type used in this book, was both an originator and a collector of types. His services to the art of printing were his design of letters, his creation of ornaments and initials, and his standardization of type sizes. His types are old-style in character and sharply cut. In 1764 and 1766 he published his *Manuel typographique*, a treatise on the history of French types and printing, on typefounding in all its details, and on what many consider his most important contribution to typography—the measurement of type by the point system.

Composed by
Stratford Publishing Services,
Brattleboro, Vermont

Printed and bound by
Quebecor World,
Martinsburg, West Virginia

Designed by
Soonyoung Kwon